1

Contemporary Topics

21st Century Skills for Academic Success

FOURTH EDITION

Helen Solórzano • Laurie Frazier

Michael Rost

SERIES EDITOR

Contemporary Topics 1, Intermediate
21st Century Skills for Academic Success
Fourth Edition

Pearson Education, 221 River Street, Hoboken, NJ 07030

Staff credits: The people who made up the **Contemporary Topics** team, representing editorial, production, design, and manufacturing, are Pietro Alongi, Claire Bowers, Stephanie Bullard, Kim Casey, Tracey Cataldo, Mindy DePalma, Dave Dickey, Pam Fishman, Niki Lee, Fabrizio Luccitti, Amy McCormick, Jennifer Raspiller, Robert Ruvo, Leigh Stolle, Paula Van Ells, and Joseph Vella.

Cover image: © Fotolia/Suchota
Text composition: MPS North America
Photo credits: See page 134

Library of Congress Cataloging-in-Publication Data
A catalog record for the print edition is available from the Library of Congress
ISBN-10: 0-13-440064-X   ISBN-13: 978-0-13-440064-8

Printed in the United States of America.
4   17

Contents

Scope and Sequence

UNIT SUBJECT AND TITLE	CORPUS-BASED VOCABULARY	NOTE-TAKING AND LISTENING FOCUS	PRONUNCIATION	DISCUSSION STRATEGY	PRESENTATION
1 **PSYCHOLOGY** Happiness	achieve data goal income method positive psychology relevant requirement research	Lecture topic and organization	Syllable stress	• **Agreeing** • Disagreeing	Present on how to be happier while showing confidence
2 **LINGUISTICS** A Time to Learn	acquisition environment factor motivation obvious period role theory	Signal questions	Rising and falling Intonation	• **Asking for opinions or ideas** • Asking for clarification or confirmation	Present on learning a language while involving the audience with questions
3 **PUBLIC HEALTH** Sleep	aspect consequence function impact injured link percent shift	Signal phrases	Signal phrases	• **Paraphrasing** • Expressing and opinion	Present on a public health issue, using signal phrases
4 **BUSINESS** Negotiating for Success	approach benefit circumstance concentrate confer conflict resolve technique	Lists	Sentence rhythm for lists and contrasting points	• **Expressing an opinion** • Asking for clarification or confirmation	Present on negotiation while speaking at a comfortable speed
5 **ART HISTORY** Modern Art	category communicate create emerge image style traditional	Definitions	Pausing between thought groups	• **Disagreeing** • Agreeing • Asking for opinions or ideas • Expressing an opinion	Present on a style of art, using visual aids
6 **ENGINEERING** Robots	attach automatically available computer obtain release specific task utilize	Examples and restatement	Contractions	• **Trying to reach a consensus** • Offering a fact or example	Present on a type of robot while persuading the audience and showing enthusiasm

UNIT SUBJECT AND TITLE	CORPUS-BASED VOCABULARY	NOTE-TAKING AND LISTENING FOCUS	PRONUNCIATION	DISCUSSION STRATEGY	PRESENTATION
7 MEDIA STUDIES Interactive Games	evidence depressed grade involve media potential	Evidence and support	Sentence rhythm that signals important ideas	• **Asking for clarification or confirmation** • Paraphrasing	Present on media use as a group
8 BIOLOGY Genetically Modified Food	consume modify normal primarily purchase retain source	Key terms	Linking unstressed words	• **Changing the topic** • Agreeing • Trying to reach a consensus	Present on food, comparing and contrasting two types
9 BUSINESS Design Thinking	diverse focus identify implement innovative participant phase revise	Description of a process	Intonation for finished and unfinished thoughts	• **Interrupting politely** • Agreeing • Expressing an opinion	Present on a design problem, using the Design Thinking process and describing the process
10 HISTORY Shackleton	credit depress finally goal job survive team	Numbers, dates, and periods of time	Linking: -ed endings	• **Keeping a discussion on topic** • Asking for opinions or ideas • Expressing an opinion	Present on an interesting or important life event, using an object or picture
11 PHILOSOPHY Ethics	community individual majority overall philosopher principle unethical	Real-world examples	Pausing that separates ideas	• **Offering a fact or example** • Expressing an opinion	Present on an ethical problem and possible decisions, applying one of the ethical approaches and pausing between ideas
12 INFORMATION TECHNOLOGY Big Data	access accurate analyze complex convert sequence	Personal stories	Sentence rhythm: Repetition	• **Keeping a discussion going** • Agreeing	Present on the pros and cons of a type of technology, using an introduction and conclusion

Acknowledgments

The series editor, authors, and publisher would like to thank the following consultants, reviewers, and teachers for offering their invaluable insights and suggestions for the fourth edition of the *Contemporary Topics* series.

Kate Reynolds, *University of Wisconsin-Eau Claire*; Kathie Gerecke, *North Shore Community College*; Jeanne Dunnett, *Central Connecticut State University*; Linda Anderson, *Washington University in St. Louis/Fontbonne University*; Sande Wu, *California State University, Fresno*; Stephanie Landon, *College of the Desert*; Jungsook Kim, *Jeungsang Language School*; Jenny Oh Kim, *Kangnamgu Daechidong*; Patty Heiser, *University of Washington*; Carrie Barnard, *Queens College*; Lori D. Giles, *University of Miami*; Nancy H. Centers, *Roger Williams University*; Lyra Riabov, *Southern New Hampshire University*; Dr. Steven Gras, *ESL Program, SUNY Plattsburgh*; series consultants Jeanette Clement and Cynthia Lennox, *Duquesne University*

New to this fourth edition, **Essential Online Resources** are available at **www.pearsonelt.com/contemporarytopics4e**, using your access code. These resources include the following:

- **VIDEO:** Watch the Lecture academic lecture videos, with or without Presentation Points, and Talk About the Topic student discussion videos are available.
- **AUDIO:** Audio clips for all audio-based Student Book activities as well as Unit Tests and Proficiency Assessment lectures are available. Audio versions of the unit lectures and student discussion are also provided. (Audio and video icons in the Student Book and Teaching Tips indicate which media is needed for each activity.)
- **STUDENT BOOK PRESENTATION SLIDES:** All units of the Student Book are available as PowerPoint® slides, allowing activities to be viewed as a class.
- **INTERACTIVE TESTS:** Teachers can administer the Unit Tests and Proficiency Assessments online.
- **PRINT RESOURCES:** Transcripts of the videos and lecture-specific Coaching Tips (covering listening, critical thinking, and note-taking) are provided along with Teaching Tips, Answer Keys, Audioscripts, Teacher and Student Evaluations Forms, Unit Tests, and Proficiency Assessments.

Introduction

The *Contemporary Topics* series provides a comprehensive approach to developing 21st century academic skills—including listening, thinking, discussion, presentation, and study skills—in order to prepare students for participation in real-life academic and professional contexts.

The overriding principle of language and skill development in the *Contemporary Topics* series is *engagement*. Activities in each unit are carefully sequenced in a way that gives students increasing involvement and self-direction of their learning. Authentic, stimulating content is introduced and developed throughout each unit so that students experience the value of understanding and exchanging contemporary ideas in a range of academic fields. *Contemporary Topics* is intended to bridge the gap between language-focused and content-focused instruction, to ready students for genuine academic and professional contexts where they will be expected to participate fully.

Each unit centers around a short academic lecture. Realistic preparation activities, focused listening tasks, personalized discussions, challenging tests, and authentic presentation assignments enable students to explore each topic deeply.

The lecture topics are drawn from a range of academic disciplines, and the lectures themselves feature engaging instructors in a variety of settings including offices, lecture halls, and classrooms, many with live student audiences.

In order to achieve the goals of content-based instruction, the *Contemporary Topics* series has developed an engaging nine-part learning methodology:

Section 1: Connect to the Topic
Estimated time: 15 minutes

This opening section invites students to activate what they already know about the unit topic by connecting the topic to their personal experiences and beliefs. Typically, students fill out a short survey and compare answers with a partner. The students then listen to a short interview providing one expert view on the unit topic. The teacher then acts as a facilitator for students to share some of their initial ideas about the topic before they explore it further.

Section 2: Build Your Vocabulary
Estimated time: 15 minutes

This section familiarizes students with some of the key content words and phrases used in the lecture. Each lecture targets 10–15 key words from the Academic Word List to ensure that students learn the core vocabulary needed for academic success.

Students read *and listen* to the target words and phrases in context so that they can better prepare for the upcoming lecture. Students then work individually or with a partner to complete exercises to ensure an initial understanding of the target lexis of the unit. A supplementary pair-work activity enables students to focus on form as they are learning new words and collocations.

Section 3: Focus Your Attention
Estimated time: 10 minutes

In this section, students learn strategies for listening actively and taking clear notes. Because a major part of "active listening" involves a readiness to deal with comprehension difficulties, this section provides specific coaching tips to help students direct their attention and gain more control of how they listen.

Tips include how to use signal words as organization cues, make lists, note definitions, link examples to main ideas, identify causes and effects, and separate points of view. A Try It section, based on a short audio extract, allows students to work on note-taking strategies before they get to the main lecture. Examples of actual notes are usually provided in this section to give students concrete "starter models" they can use in the classroom.

Section 4: Watch the Lecture
Estimated time: 20–30 minutes

As the central section of each unit, Watch the Lecture allows for two full listening cycles, one to focus on "top-down listening" strategies (Listen for Main Ideas) and one to focus on "bottom-up listening" strategies (Listen for Details).

In keeping with the principles of content-based instruction, students are provided with several layers of support. In the Think About It section, students are guided to activate concepts and vocabulary they have studied earlier in the unit.

The lecture can be viewed as a video or just listened to on audio. The video version includes the speaker's Presentation Points.

Section 5: Hear the Language
Estimated time: 10 minutes

This section focuses on "bottom-up" listening strategies and pronunciation. In this section, students hear ten short extracts taken from the actual lecture and perform a noticing task. The task helps students perceive sound reductions and assimilations, learn to hear language as "thought groups" and pauses, and tune in to function of stress and intonation.

Students then work in pairs to practice their pronunciation, adapting the phonology point that was learned in the listening task.

Section 6: Talk About the Topic
Estimated time: 15 minutes

Here students gain valuable discussion skills as they talk about the content of the lectures. Discussion skills are an important part of academic success, and most students benefit from structured practice with these skills. In this activity, students first listen to a short "model discussion" involving native and nonnative speakers, and identify the speaking strategies and gambits that are used. They then attempt to use some of those strategies in their own discussion groups.

The discussion strategies modeled and explained across the units include the following:

- Agreeing
- Asking for clarification or confirmation
- Asking for opinions or ideas
- Disagreeing
- Expressing an opinion
- Keeping a discussion on topic
- Offering a fact or example
- Trying to reach a consensus
- Paraphrasing

Section 7: Review Your Notes

Estimated time: 10 minutes

Using notes for review and discussion is an important study skill that is developed in this section. Research has shown that the value of note-taking for memory building is realized *primarily* when note-takers review their notes and attempt to reconstruct the content.

In this activity, students are guided in reviewing the content of the unit, clarifying concepts, and preparing for the Unit Test. Abbreviated examples of actual notes are provided to help students compare and improve their own note-taking skills.

Section 8: Take the Unit Test and Proficiency Assessment

Estimated time: 15 minutes each

Taking the **Unit Test** completes the study cycle of the unit: preparation for the lecture, listening to the lecture, review of the content, and assessment.

The Unit Test, contained only in the Teacher's Pack, is administered by the teacher and then completed in class, using the accompanying audio. The tests in *Contemporary Topics* are intended to be challenging—to motivate students to learn the material thoroughly. The format features an answer sheet with choices. The question "stem" is provided on audio only. Test-taking skills include verbatim recall, paraphrasing, inferencing, and synthesizing information from different parts of the lecture.

The **Proficiency Assessment** is an audio lecture and ten multiple-choice questions designed to give students practice listening and taking standardized tests. It, too, is found only in the Teacher's Pack and should be administered by the teacher and completed in class using the accompanying audio.

Section 9: Express Your Ideas

Estimated time: Will vary by class size

This final section creates a natural extension of the unit topic to areas that are relevant to students. Students go through a guided process of preparing, practicing, and presenting on a topic of personal interest. Students are also given guidance in listening to other students' presentations and providing helpful feedback.

A supplementary Teacher's Pack (TP) contains teaching tips, transcripts, answer keys, tests, and teacher evaluation forms.

We hope you will enjoy using this course. While the *Contemporary Topics* series provides an abundance of learning activities and media, the key to making the course work in your classroom is student engagement and commitment. For content-based learning to be effective, students need to become *active* learners. This involves thinking critically, guessing, interacting, offering ideas, collaborating, questioning, and responding. The authors and editors of *Contemporary Topics* have created a rich framework for encouraging students to become active, successful learners. We hope that we have also provided you, the teacher, with tools for becoming an active guide to the students in their learning.

Michael Rost
SERIES EDITOR

Learning Path

ACTIVATION SECTIONS 1 / 2 / 3

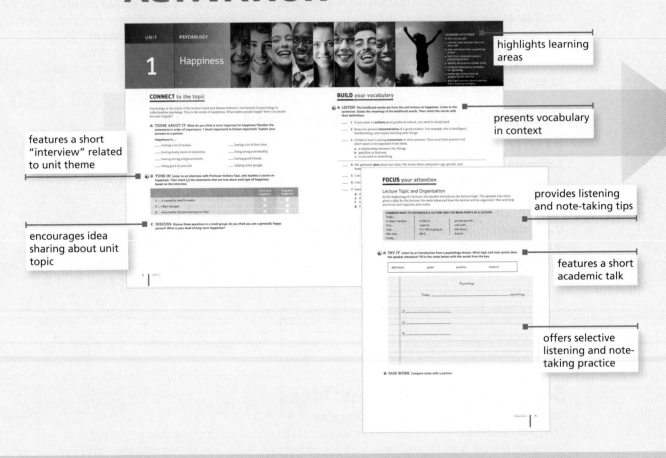

- features a short "interview" related to unit theme
- encourages idea sharing about unit topic
- highlights learning areas
- presents vocabulary in context
- provides listening and note-taking tips
- features a short academic talk
- offers selective listening and note-taking practice

EXPRESSION SECTION 9

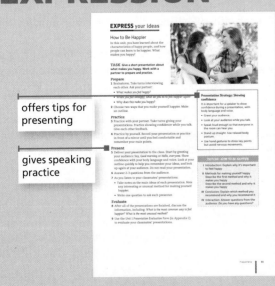

- offers tips for presenting
- gives speaking practice
- allows opportunity to assess presentations

PROCESSING SECTIONS 4 / 5 / 6

encourages anticipation of lecture topic

features an academic lecture and requires gist and intensive listening, and active note-taking

features lecture extracts that demonstrate phonology points

prompts pronunciation practice

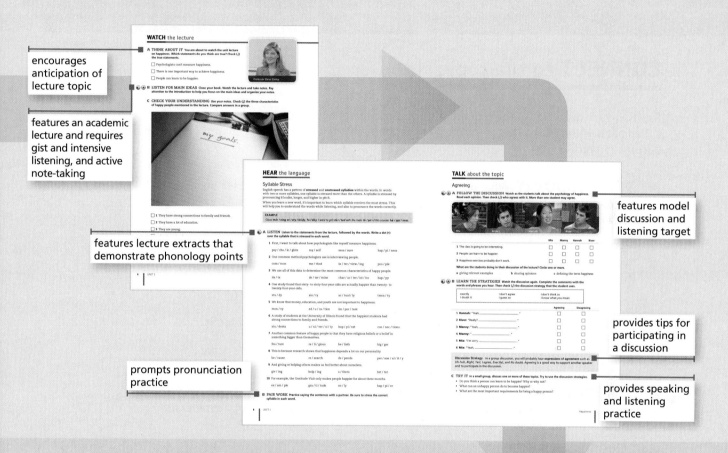

features model discussion and listening target

provides tips for participating in a discussion

provides speaking and listening practice

ASSESSMENT SECTIONS 7 / 8

provides opportunity to revise notes

allows demonstration of content mastery

features a short academic lecture and offers assessment within a high-stakes listening environment

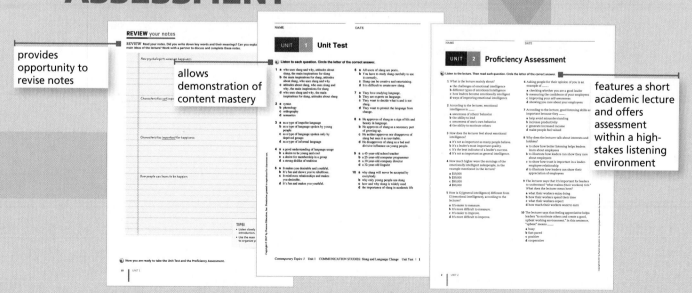

1 Happiness

CONNECT to the topic

Psychology is the study of the human mind and human behavior. One branch of psychology is called *positive psychology*. This is the study of happiness. What makes people happy? How can people become happier?

A THINK ABOUT IT What do you think is most important for happiness? Number the statements in order of importance: 1 (most important) to 8 (least important). Explain your answers to a partner.

Happiness is ...

_____ having a lot of money.

_____ having many years of education.

_____ having strong religious beliefs.

_____ being good at your job.

_____ having a lot of free time.

_____ being young and healthy.

_____ having good friends.

_____ helping other people.

B TUNE IN Listen to an interview with Professor Stefano Tassi, who teaches a course on happiness. Then check (√) the statements that are true about each type of happiness, based on the interview.

	Short-term happiness	Long-term happiness
1 ... is caused by specific events.	☐	☐
2 ... often changes.	☐	☐
3 ... stays mostly the same during our lives.	☐	☐

C DISCUSS Discuss these questions in a small group: *Do you think you are a generally happy person? What is your level of long-term happiness?*

LEARNING OUTCOMES

In this unit you will:

- note the topic and main ideas of a short talk
- note main ideas from a psychology lecture
- fact-check statements about a psychology lecture
- identify and practice syllable stress
- recognize and practice strategies for **agreeing**
- review your lecture notes to prepare for the unit test
- give a presentation about happiness while showing confidence

BUILD your vocabulary

A LISTEN The boldfaced words are from the unit lecture on happiness. Listen to the sentences. Guess the meanings of the boldfaced words. Then match the words with their definitions.

_____ 1 If you want to **achieve** good grades in school, you need to study hard.

_____ 2 Rosa has several **characteristics** of a good student. For example, she is intelligent, hardworking, and enjoys learning new things.

_____ 3 Children have a strong **connection** to their parents. They need their parents and don't want to be separated from them.

    a a relationship between two things
    b qualities or features
    c to succeed at something

_____ 4 We gathered **data** about our class. We wrote down everyone's age, gender, and hometown.

_____ 5 I set a **goal** for myself: I want to go to graduate school and become a psychologist.

_____ 6 I feel a lot of **gratitude** toward my parents. I'm thankful for what they've done for me.

_____ 7 Jawad has a good **income**. He has enough money to buy a house and live comfortably.

    d the feeling of being thankful
    e money that a person earns
    f information or facts
    g something you hope to do in the future

_____ 8 To check a child's health, doctors usually **measure** the child's height and weight. They want to make sure the child's size is normal and healthy.

_____ 9 One **method** psychologists use to help unhappy people is to talk to them about their feelings. Another is to give them medication.

_____ 10 You can see a child's **personality** at a young age. Some children are quiet and shy, while others are outgoing and friendly.

  h a way of doing something
  i the type of person you are, shown by how you behave, feel, or think
  j find out the size, weight, or amount of something

_____ 11 I'm getting a degree in math. I don't need to study psychology because it isn't **relevant** to my major.

_____ 12 A graduate degree is a **requirement** for becoming a psychology professor. You must have it in order to teach at a university.

_____ 13 My professor is doing **research** on the psychology of happiness. She's studying happy people to find out what makes them happy.

_____ 14 She has many **strengths** that help her to be a good psychologist. For example, she works well with other people and likes to learn new things.

  k something that is needed
  l good qualities of a person
  m the detailed study of a subject in order to learn new facts about it
  n related to a subject

B PAIR WORK Work with a partner. Notice the boldfaced words. Circle the best word to complete the sentences. Take turns saying the sentences.

1 My sister has a positive **attitude** (with / about) life.

2 I have a strong **connection** (from / to) my family.

3 Psychologists gather **data** (on / in) their patients.

4 My final grade in psychology class will **depend** (on / of) how I do on the final exam.

5 These exercises were **developed** (by / to) our teacher to help us learn.

6 A survey is one method that psychologists use to **find** (on / out) people's opinions.

7 Frank achieved his **goal** (to / of) graduating from college.

8 I feel **gratitude** (with / toward) my teachers.

9 I earn **income** (from / in) a part-time job.

10 Can we change our **level** (in / of) happiness?

11 English is a **requirement** (with / for) my major.

12 Psychologists did **research** (of / on) happiness.

FOCUS your attention

Lecture Topic and Organization

At the beginning of a lecture, the speaker introduces the lecture topic. The speaker also often gives a plan for the lecture: the main ideas and how the lecture will be organized. This will help you focus and organize your notes.

COMMON WAYS TO INTRODUCE A LECTURE AND THE MAIN POINTS OF A LECTURE

Today ...	I'd like to ...	get started with ...
In today's lecture, ...	I want to ...	start with ...
First, ...	I'm / We're going to ...	talk about ...
Then ...	We'll ...	look at ...
After that, ...		
Finally, ...		

A TRY IT Listen to an introduction from a psychology lecture. What topic and main points does the speaker introduce? Fill in the notes below with the words from the box.

definition	goals	positive	research

Psychology

Today: _____ psychology

1) _____

2) _____

3) _____

B PAIR WORK Compare notes with a partner.

WATCH the lecture

Professor Dana Dailey

A THINK ABOUT IT You are about to watch the unit lecture on happiness. Which statements do you think are true? Check (√) the true statements.

☐ Psychologists can't measure happiness.

☐ There is one important way to achieve happiness.

☐ People can learn to be happier.

B LISTEN FOR MAIN IDEAS Close your book. Watch the lecture and take notes. Pay attention to the introduction to help you focus on the main ideas and organize your notes.

C CHECK YOUR UNDERSTANDING Use your notes. Check (√) the three characteristics of happy people mentioned in the lecture. Compare answers in a group.

☐ **1** They have strong connections to family and friends.

☐ **2** They have a lot of education.

☐ **3** They are young.

☐ **4** They have a lot of money.

☐ **5** They have religious or other beliefs.

☐ **6** They are married.

☐ **7** They set goals for themselves.

🔊 ⏹ **D** **LISTEN FOR DETAILS** Close your book. Watch the lecture again. Add details to your notes and correct any mistakes.

E **CHECK YOUR UNDERSTANDING** Use your notes to decide if the statements are *T* (true) or *F* (false), based on the lecture. Correct the false statements.

_____ **1** Psychologists measure happiness by interviewing and gathering data on people.

_____ **2** One study found that 60- to 64-year-olds have the same level of happiness as 20- to 24-year-olds.

_____ **3** Having religious or other beliefs helps people feel that their lives have meaning.

_____ **4** Happy people set goals that are easy to achieve.

_____ **5** Research shows that people can easily change their personalities.

_____ **6** Positive psychologists develop exercises to help people feel happier.

_____ **7** In the Gratitude Visit, people give a gift to someone they want to thank.

_____ **8** The Gratitude Visit helps people feel more connected to others.

_____ **9** Positive psychologists believe that happiness exercises help people feel a lot happier.

HEAR the language

Syllable Stress

English speech has a pattern of **stressed** and **unstressed syllables** within the words. In words with two or more syllables, one syllable is stressed more than the others. A syllable is stressed by pronouncing it louder, longer, and higher in pitch.

When you learn a new word, it's important to learn which syllable receives the most stress. This will help you to understand the words while listening, and also to pronounce the words correctly.

EXAMPLE

Good mor / ning ev / ery / bo dy. To / day, I want to get star / ted with the main to / pic of this course: ha / ppi / ness.

A LISTEN Listen to the statements from the lecture, followed by the words. Write a dot (•) over the syllable that is stressed in each word.

1 First, I want to talk about how psychologists like myself measure happiness.

psy / cho / lo / gists   my / self   mea / sure   hap / pi / ness

2 One common method psychologists use is interviewing people.

com / mon   me / thod   in / ter / view / ing   peo / ple

3 We use all of this data to determine the most common characteristics of happy people.

da / ta   de / ter / mine   char / ac / ter / ist / ics   hap / py

4 One study found that sixty- to sixty-four-year-olds are actually happier than twenty- to twenty-four-year-olds.

stu / dy   six / ty   ac / tual / ly   twen / ty

5 We know that money, education, and youth are not important to happiness.

mon / ey   ed / u / ca / tion   im / por / tant

6 A study of students at the University of Illinois found that the happiest students had strong connections to family and friends.

stu / dents   u / ni / ver / si / ty   hap / pi / est   con / nec / tions

7 Another common feature of happy people is that they have religious beliefs or a belief in something bigger than themselves.

fea / ture   re / li / gious   be / liefs   big / ger

8 This is because research shows that happiness depends a lot on our personality.

be / cause   re / search   de / pends   per / son / al / it / y

9 And giving or helping others makes us feel better about ourselves.

giv / ing   help / ing   o / thers   bet / ter

10 For example, the Gratitude Visit only makes people happier for about three months.

ex / am / ple   gra / ti / tude   on / ly   hap / pi / er

B PAIR WORK Practice saying the sentences with a partner. Be sure to stress the correct syllable in each word.

TALK about the topic

Agreeing

A FOLLOW THE DISCUSSION Watch as the students talk about the psychology of happiness. Read each opinion. Then check (√) who agrees with it. More than one student may agree.

Mia   Manny   Hannah   River

	Mia	Manny	Hannah	River
1 The class is going to be interesting.	☐	☐	☐	☐
2 People can learn to be happier.	☐	☐	☐	☐
3 Happiness exercises probably don't work.	☐	☐	☐	☐

What are the students doing in their discussion of the lecture? Circle one or more.

a giving relevant examples   **b** sharing opinions   **c** defining the term *happiness*

B LEARN THE STRATEGIES Watch the discussion again. Complete the comments with the words and phrases you hear. Then check (√) the discussion strategy that the student uses.

exactly	I don't agree	I don't think so
I doubt it	I guess so	I know what you mean

	Agreeing	Disagreeing
1 Hannah: "Yeah, _____ ."	☐	☐
2 River: "Really? _____ ."	☐	☐
3 Manny: "Yeah, _____ ."	☐	☐
4 Manny: " _____ ."	☐	☐
5 Mia: "I'm sorry. _____ ."	☐	☐
6 Mia: "Yeah, _____ ."	☐	☐

Discussion Strategy In a group discussion, you will probably hear **expressions of agreement** such as *Uh-huh, Right, Yes!, I agree, Exactly!,* and *No doubt.* Agreeing is a good way to support another speaker and to participate in the discussion.

C TRY IT In a small group, discuss one or more of these topics. Try to use the discussion strategies.

- Do you think a person can learn to be happier? Why or why not?
- What can an unhappy person do to become happier?
- What are the most important requirements for being a happy person?

REVIEW your notes

REVIEW Read your notes. Did you write down key words and their meanings? Can you explain the main ideas of the lecture? Work with a partner to discuss and complete these notes.

How psychologists measure happiness:

Characteristics <u>not</u> important for happiness:

Characteristics <u>important</u> for happiness:

How people can learn to be happier:

TIPS!

- Listen closely to the lecturer's introduction.
- Use the main ideas you hear to organize your notes.

 Now you are ready to take the Unit Test and the Proficiency Assessment.

EXPRESS your ideas

How to Be Happier

In this unit, you have learned about the characteristics of happy people, and how people can learn to be happier. What makes you happy?

TASK Give a short presentation about what makes you happy. Work with a partner to prepare and practice.

Prepare

1 Brainstorm. Take turns interviewing each other. Ask your partner:

- *What makes you feel happy?*
- *When you feel unhappy, what do you do to feel happier again?*
- *Why does this make you happy?*

2 Choose two ways that you make yourself happier. Make an outline.

Practice

3 Practice with your partner. Take turns giving your presentations. Practice showing confidence while you talk. Give each other feedback.

4 Practice by yourself. Record your presentation or practice in front of a mirror until you feel comfortable and remember your main points.

Present

5 Deliver your presentation to the class. Start by greeting your audience: Say, *Good morning* or *Hello, everyone.* Show confidence with your body language and voice. Look at your outline quickly to help you remember your ideas, and look up again at your audience. Do not read your presentation.

6 Answer 2–3 questions from the audience.

7 As you listen to your classmates' presentations:

- Take notes on the main ideas of each presentation. Note any interesting or unusual method for making yourself happier.
- Write one question to ask each presenter.

Evaluate

8 After all of the presentations are finished, discuss the information, including: *What is the most common way to feel happier? What is the most unusual method?*

9 Use the *Unit 1 Presentation Evaluation Form* (in Appendix C) to evaluate your classmates' presentations.

Presentation Strategy: Showing confidence

It is important for a speaker to show confidence during a presentation, with body language and voice.

- Greet your audience.
- Look at your audience while you talk.
- Speak loud enough so that everyone in the room can hear you.
- Stand up straight. Use relaxed body posture.
- Use hand gestures to stress key points but avoid nervous movements.

OUTLINE: HOW TO BE HAPPIER

I Introduction: Explain why it's important to feel happy

II Methods for making yourself happy
Describe the first method and why it makes you happy
Describe the second method and why it makes you happy

III Conclusion: Explain which method you recommend and why you recommend it

IV Interaction: Answer questions from the audience: *Do you have any questions?*

2 A Time to Learn

CONNECT to the topic

Linguistics is the study of language. One area of linguistics is the study of how people learn language. As babies, we all learned our native language from people around us. Many people learn a second language as children or adults.

A THINK ABOUT IT Work in a small group. Read the statements. Check (√) your opinion. Compare answers with a partner.

	Strongly disagree	Disagree	Agree	Strongly agree
• Children learn new languages easily.	☐	☐	☐	☐
• Adults can never learn a new language well.	☐	☐	☐	☐
• A good way to learn a language is to live where it's spoken.	☐	☐	☐	☐
• Some languages are very difficult to learn.	☐	☐	☐	☐
• Learning new languages is easy for some people.	☐	☐	☐	☐
• There are benefits (helpful results) of learning new languages.	☐	☐	☐	☐

Share your opinions with the group. Use examples from your experience to explain your opinions.

B TUNE IN Listen to an interview with linguist Julia Chintha, talking about bilingualism. Then check (√) the statements as *True* or *False*.

	True	False
1 More than 75 percent of people in the world are bilingual.	☐	☐
2 In Indonesia, Indonesian is used as a common language at school and work.	☐	☐
3 One in four people in the world speak Chinese as a native language.	☐	☐
4 English is the most widely used second language.	☐	☐
5 In the United States, about 25 percent of native English speakers are bilingual.	☐	☐

C DISCUSS Discuss these questions in a small group: *Which languages do you use in your everyday life? Why are you learning English?* Explain your reasons.

BUILD your vocabulary

A LISTEN The boldfaced words are from the unit lecture on language acquisition. Listen to each passage. Read along. Then circle the best meaning of the boldfaced word.

There are several different **theories** about how people learn language. But no one really knows how language **acquisition** happens.

1 A **theory** is an explanation of something that _____.

   a might or might not be correct   **b** is definitely correct   **c** is completely wrong

2 Language **acquisition** is _____ a language.

   a teaching   **b** speaking   **c** learning

This semester I'm taking an English language class. Next year I'm going to Australia, so I have a lot of **motivation** to study. English is a **critical** skill that I need to learn before my trip.

3 **Motivation** is the _____ you want to do something.

   a time when   **b** reason why   **c** place where

4 A **critical** skill is a skill that is _____.

   a easy to learn   **b** very important   **c** not useful

During the first year of life, babies go through a **period** called babbling. During this time, the baby makes sounds but can't say words yet. Linguists think that babbling plays an important **role** in language learning.

5 A **period** is _____.

   a a length of time   **b** a sound   **c** an age

6 Playing a **role** in language learning means _____ language learning.

   a having a problem with   **b** giving a reason for   **c** being a part of

Why do so many people study English? There are many **factors** that make it a popular subject. One **obvious** reason is for education. Many students need to study textbooks that are in English.

7 A **factor** is _____ that affects a situation.

   a the only thing   **b** one of several things   **c** the most important thing

8 An **obvious** reason is a reason that is _____ .

   a easy to notice   **b** hard to understand   **c** interesting to know about

---

I think that living in another country is the **ideal** way to learn a new language. You're in an **environment** where you have to speak the language all the time, so your **brain** begins to take in the new language.

9 The **ideal** way to do something is the _____ way to do it.

   a most complicated   **b** most expensive   **c** best possible

10 Our **environment** is _____ .

   a how we do things   **b** the time needed to   **c** the conditions around us
                                 get somewhere

11 The **brain** is the part of the body that _____ .

   a controls how you think   **b** turns food into energy   **c** takes air in

B **PAIR WORK** Work with a partner. Notice the boldfaced words. Reorder the words and write the complete sentence. Take turns saying the sentences.

1 Today's **lecture** is (acquisition / language / **on** / second).

_____

2 Your thoughts and movements are (brain / **by** / **controlled** / your).

_____

3 Early childhood is (a / **for** / critical / learning / **time**).

_____

4 In my English class, we're (**an** / **environment** / all-English / **in**).

_____

5 Hard work is (**factor** / important / an / **for** / doing well) at school.

_____

6 A long drive is (the / to **listen** / ideal / **to** a language learning podcast / time).

_____

7 Hussein has (English / learning / **motivation** / strong / **for**).

_____

8 One obvious (**for** learning / **reason** / a new language / **is**) to travel.

_____

9 I studied (for / **period** / French / a / short / **of** time).

_____

10 Parents have (an / **in** / **role** / their children's lives / important).

_____

11 We read an article (about / language learning / **theories** / **on**).

_____

FOCUS your attention

Signal Questions

A speaker often uses a question to focus listeners' attention. Sometimes the speaker does not want an answer to the question. Instead, the speaker uses a signal question to introduce a new point or to signal important information. These are usually called *rhetorical questions*.

REGULAR QUESTIONS

When asking a regular question, the speaker usually ...
- stops talking.
- looks for raised hands.
- calls on someone to give the answer.

RHETORICAL QUESTIONS

When asking a rhetorical question, the speaker often ...
- pauses briefly.
- looks at the listeners directly.
- continues speaking without waiting for an answer.

A TRY IT Listen to an excerpt from a lecture on linguistics. What information does the speaker signal with rhetorical questions? Complete the notes below as you listen.

Linguistics: Learning Language

1 Babies: How do _____?

       – hear language

       – ready at birth

Why do _____?

B PAIR WORK Compare notes with a partner.

WATCH the lecture

Professor Brian Murphy

A **THINK ABOUT IT** You are about to watch the unit lecture on second language acquisition. What do you think is the most important factor for learning a second language? Check (✓) one factor.

- ☐ intelligence
- ☐ a good teacher
- ☐ age
- ☐ the learning environment
- ☐ other: _____

B **LISTEN FOR MAIN IDEAS** Close your book. Watch the lecture and take notes. Be sure to note the main factors in language learning.

C **CHECK YOUR UNDERSTANDING** Use your notes. Choose the best answer, based on the lecture.

1 The professor compares himself to Steven, who is _____ .
- **a** a six-year-old boy
- **b** a sixteen-year-old teenager
- **c** a sixty-year-old man

2 The critical period is a time when _____ .
- **a** a child can learn language very easily
- **b** teenagers stop learning language
- **c** adults have difficulty learning language

3 The critical period _____ .
- **a** has a small effect on language learning
- **b** is one of several factors in language learning
- **c** is the most important factor in language learning

4 Other factors for successful language learning are _____ .
- **a** teachers, textbooks, and homework
- **b** intelligence, personality, and study habits
- **c** environment, attitude, and motivation

5 The main point of the lecture is that _____ .
- **a** adults can't learn a new language
- **b** age is not an important factor in language learning
- **c** there are several factors that affect language learning

D **LISTEN FOR DETAILS** Close your book. Watch the lecture again. Add details to your notes and correct any mistakes.

E CHECK YOUR UNDERSTANDING Use your notes. Read the statements and check (√) the correct name, based on the lecture. Some statements may be true for both people.

	Steven	Professor	
1	☐	☐	speaks English now.
2	☐	☐	is learning Chinese.
3	☐	☐	recently started studying a new language.
4	☐	☐	is in the critical period for language learning.
5	☐	☐	is in an environment where he hears the new language all the time.
6	☐	☐	could learn better in a different environment.
7	☐	☐	feels embarrassed when he makes mistakes in the new language.
8	☐	☐	wants to learn the new language to talk with his friends.

HEAR the language

Rising and Falling Intonation

English speech has a pattern of **rising and falling intonation**. Intonation is the pitch (high and low) of the voice. The pitch can rise slightly (go up) or fall (go down).

One use of intonation is to signal when an idea is finished. Rising intonation shows that the speaker is not finished and plans to say more. Falling intonation shows that a speaker has completed an idea.

Learning to notice intonation in sentences will help you become a better listener.

EXAMPLE

It's easier for kids to learn than it is for adults.

A LISTEN Listen to the statements from the lecture. Note the speaker's intonation over the boldfaced words. Write an up arrow (↗) when intonation rises and a down arrow (↘) when intonation falls.

1 And then we'll talk about other factors, such as the learning **environment**, **attitude**, and **motivation**.

2 Now, from the show of **hands**, I see that many of you've had your own personal experience with language **learning**. And I have recently, **too**.

3 And so I've been going to **class**, you know, listening to language **CDs**, and I'm **learning**, but it's **tough**. It's tough to learn a new **language**.

4 This is so **unfair**. We've both been **studying** a new language for the same amount of **time**, but he's learning it so much more **quickly**.

5 Many people, including linguist Robert **DeKeyser**, would say no, you have to look at other **factors**.

6 Now when I was watching Steven in the **classroom**, playing with his **friends**, it was clear he didn't feel at all embarrassed about his English language **abilities**.

7 You know, he can't speak perfectly **yet**, but when he made a mistake, he didn't **care**, and neither did his **friends**. They just kept on **playing**.

8 So clearly, a person's attitude about **learning** is very important in acquiring a second **language**.

9 So we're both motivated to **learn**, but perhaps my motivation isn't quite as **strong**.

10 As for **me**, I'm not ready to give up on Chinese just **yet**!

B PAIR WORK Practice saying the sentences with a partner. Be sure to use the correct rising or falling intonation.

TALK about the topic

Asking for Opinions or Ideas

A FOLLOW THE DISCUSSION Watch as the students talk about the critical period theory. Read each comment. Then check (√) who makes the comment.

Molly   Rob   Alana   Ayman

	Molly	Rob	Alana	Ayman
1 "The big thing is that it's harder to learn a language if you're an adult, right?"	☐	☐	☐	☐
2 "I came to the United States from Russia as a teenager."	☐	☐	☐	☐
3 "Oh, really? I thought kids learned easily."	☐	☐	☐	☐
4 "To me, the critical period explains a lot."	☐	☐	☐	☐

What are the students doing in their discussion of the lecture? Circle one or more.

a giving relevant examples   **b** sharing opinions   **c** reviewing the main points

B LEARN THE STRATEGIES Watch the discussion again. Complete the comments with the phrases you hear. Then check (√) the discussion strategy that the student uses.

how so	what does everyone think	what other factors	what about you

	Asking for clarification or confirmation	Asking for opinions or ideas
1 Rob: "OK, so _____ about this 'critical period' theory?"	☐	☐
2 Molly: "_____?"	☐	☐
3 Rob: "Really? _____?"	☐	☐
4 Rob: "_____? What was it like for you?"	☐	☐

Discussion Strategy Everyone appreciates being asked about their thoughts on a subject. By **asking for opinions or ideas,** you can bring up new ideas and help others become involved in the discussion. It's easy to ask, *What do you think?* The next step—listening—is where your learning begins!

C TRY IT In a small group, discuss one or more of these topics. Try to use the discussion strategies.

- In your experience, how does the critical period affect language learning?
- How do factors such as attitude, environment, and motivation affect language learning?
- How can you be a successful language learner?

REVIEW your notes

REVIEW Read your notes. Did you write down key words and meanings? Can you explain the main ideas? Work with a partner to discuss the list of terms from the lecture. Then complete these notes.

Term	Def.	How it affects Steven (ex.)	How it affects professor (ex.)
critical period			
language learning environment			
attitude about language learning			
motivation for language learning			

TIP!
Remember: Rhetorical questions are meant to make you think about a topic. You don't need to answer the question aloud.

Now you are ready to take the Unit Test and the Proficiency Assessment.

EXPRESS your ideas

Learning a Language

In this unit, you have learned about how environment, attitude, and motivation affect language learning. What strategies do you find helpful for language learning?

TASK **Give a short presentation with suggestions for learning a language. Work in a group to prepare and practice.**

Prepare

1 Brainstorm. Each group member should choose one language skill to present about. Choose from this list:

> Giving presentations   Pronunciation (Speaking
> Grammar   clearly)
> Learning vocabulary   Reading
> Listening   Writing
> Making conversation   Your idea: _____

2 In your group, discuss these questions:

- *What is difficult about learning this language skill?*
- *What are the best methods to improve this skill?*

3 Choose three suggestions for improving this skill. Make an outline.

Practice

4 Practice with your group. Take turns giving your presentations. Practice involving your audience with questions. Give each other feedback.

5 Practice by yourself. Record your presentation or practice in front of a mirror until you feel comfortable and remember your main points.

Present

6 Deliver your presentation to the class. Ask questions to involve your audience. Look at your outline quickly to help you remember your ideas, and look up again at your audience. Do not read your presentation.

7 Answer 2–3 questions from the audience.

8 As you listen to your classmates' presentations:

- Take notes on the main ideas of each presentation. Note a useful or interesting suggestion for improving your language skills.
- Write one question to ask each presenter.

Evaluate

9 After all of the presentations are finished, discuss the information, including: *What is the most useful suggestion for improving your language skills? What is the most interesting or unusual suggestion for improving?*

10 Use the *Unit 2 Presentation Evaluation Form* (in Appendix C) to evaluate your classmates' presentations.

Presentation Strategy: Involving your audience with questions

It is important to get the attention of your audience and keep everyone interested in your presentation. One way to do this is to ask questions. You can ask questions to:

- get the audience thinking about your topic: *What do you know about … ?*
- connect your audience to the topic: *How many of you … ?*
- get the audience's opinions on your topic: *What do you think … ?*
- introduce a new topic: *What does this mean?*

When you ask questions, be sure to use the correct intonation. Make eye contact with your audience. Wait and listen for responses. Repeat or summarize the responses and make brief comments.

OUTLINE: LEARNING A LANGUAGE

I Introduction

    Ask a question to introduce your topic

    Tell the audience which language skill you will talk about

II Suggestions for improving the language skill

    Explain one method for improving with details about how to do it

    Explain a second method for improving with details about how to do it

    Explain a third method for improving with details about how to do it

III Conclusion: Recommend the best way to improve and why you like it

IV Interaction: Answer questions from the audience

3 Sleep

CONNECT to the topic

Public health is the study of the health of people in a community. Public health professionals use education and health services to help people have a healthier lifestyle. For example, a public health professional may teach people how to eat healthy food, get enough exercise, and develop good sleep habits.

A THINK ABOUT IT Read the statements. Circle the number below the word that describes how often each statement applies to you. Then add the numbers to calculate your score. Compare answers with a partner.

	Always	Usually	Sometimes	Never
• I stay up very late at night.	4	3	2	1
• I go to bed as soon as I feel tired.	1	2	3	4
• I need an alarm clock to wake up.	4	3	2	1
• I feel tired when I wake up.	4	3	2	1
• I fall asleep during the day.	4	3	2	1
• I get enough sleep most nights.	1	2	3	4
• I sleep more on weekends than on weekdays.	4	3	2	1
• I wake up feeling rested in the morning.	1	2	3	4
Total _____	= _____	+ _____	+ _____	+ _____

Scoring: **8–16:** You usually get enough sleep.

17–24: You should try to get more sleep.

25–32: You definitely need more sleep.

B TUNE IN Listen to an interview with Dr. David Trujillo, talking about sleep. Then complete the statement by circling all correct answers.

The doctor mentions sleep problems caused by _____.

a medical problems   **b** drinking coffee   **c** technology   **d** electronic screens   **e** noise

C DISCUSS Discuss these questions in a small group: *When do you have sleep problems? What causes those problems? What can you do if you have trouble falling asleep?*

BUILD your vocabulary

A LISTEN The boldfaced words are from the unit lecture on sleep. Listen to each sentence. Then circle the best meaning of the boldfaced word.

1 Health problems can affect every **aspect** of your life. They can affect your level of happiness, your success in school or at work, and your relationships.

   a time   **b** trouble   **c** part

2 Feeling tired in the morning is a **consequence** of going to bed late.

   a result of an action   **b** reason for an action   **c** argument in favor of an action

3 I can't **function** if I don't get enough sleep. I have trouble thinking the next day.

   a work   **b** sleep   **c** relax

4 Taking the sleeping pills had an **immediate** effect. I fell asleep in 10 minutes.

   a slow   **b** instant   **c** difficult

5 Staying up late last night had an **impact** on me today. I've been very tired all day.

   a effect   **b** problem   **c** source

6 I **injured** myself when I fell down the stairs, and now my foot hurts when I walk.

   a helped   **b** hurt   **c** broke

7 There is a **link** between cigarette smoking and cancer: Smoking causes cancer.

   a cost   **b** connection   **c** problem

8 Older people are **more likely** than other adults to have sleep problems. They have more trouble falling asleep and wake up more often in the night.

   a with greater possibility   **b** with more trouble   **c** with greater difficulty

9 Fifty **percent** of teenagers say they don't sleep enough. That's one out of every two!

   a a lot of   **b** of each hundred   **c** a few

10 I **realized** I was tired when I fell asleep on the bus and missed my stop. Before that happened, I'd thought I was getting enough sleep.

    a thought about how   **b** understood   **c** forgot

11 My father works the night **shift**, from 11:00 P.M. until 8:00 A.M., and sleeps during the day.

    a work period   **b** vacation   **c** day off

12 **Sleep deprivation** is a serious problem—without enough rest, people become sick.

    a a lot of rest   **b** a lack of sleep   **c** a short nap

13 I **suffer** from serious headaches. My head hurts for hours, and I can't go to work.

    a enjoy   **b** try   **c** am sick with

B **PAIR WORK** Work with a partner. Student A: Read aloud sentences 1–3 in Column 1. Student B: Listen and complete the sentences in Column 2. Notice the boldfaced words. Switch roles for 4–7.

COLUMN 1	COLUMN 2
1 My grandmother **suffers from** sleep deprivation.	**1** My grandmother **suffers** _____ sleep deprivation.
2 It's difficult to function when you have a **lack of sleep**.	**2** It's difficult to function when you have a **lack** _____ **sleep**.
3 Sleep deprivation doesn't always have an **immediate effect on** people.	**3** Sleep deprivation doesn't always have an **immediate effect** _____ people.
4 Students who **stay up** late may get bad grades.	**4** Students who **stay** _____ late may get bad grades.
5 Compared to adults, children are more **likely to** go to sleep early.	**5** Compared to adults, children are more **likely** _____ go to sleep early.
6 Many people are **injured in** car accidents each year.	**6** Many people are **injured** _____ car accidents each year.
7 Nurses **work in shifts**: days, evenings, or nights.	**7** Nurses **work** _____ **shifts**: days, evenings, or nights.

FOCUS your attention

Signal Phrases

Speakers can use signal phrases to introduce a new point, to give an example, or to emphasize an important point. Listening for these phrases can help you understand what is coming next. This will help you better organize your notes.

PHRASES THAT INTRODUCE A NEW POINT

Now ...

Let's start with ...

First, ...

Next, ...

In addition ...

Finally, ...

PHRASES THAT GIVE AN EXAMPLE

One example is ...

For example, ...

For instance, ...

This is illustrated ...

Let's look at an example ...

PHRASES THAT EMPHASIZE A POINT

In fact, ...

It's clear that ...

Interesting, huh?

A TRY IT Listen to an excerpt from a lecture on public health. What phrase(s) does the speaker use to signal important information? Circle the phrase(s) you hear.

Public Health: Sleep

I. Sleep — children

   more sleep than adults

   e.g. newborn — 16 hrs. / day

   Sleep = important!!

Signal Phrases

1 First / Now

2 For example / For instance

3 It's clear that / In fact

B PAIR WORK Compare answers with a partner.

WATCH the lecture

A THINK ABOUT IT You are about to watch the unit lecture on the effects of sleep deprivation. Answer the following question: *What happens to you when you don't get enough sleep at night?*

_____

_____

Professor Ruth Brooks-Hall

B LISTEN FOR MAIN IDEAS Close your book. Watch the lecture and take notes.

C CHECK YOUR UNDERSTANDING Use your notes. Circle the five effects of sleep deprivation mentioned in the lecture. Then write them in the two categories below.

car accidents	lower grades in school
divorce and family problems	mistakes at work
emotional stress	serious health problems
financial trouble	weight gain

Immediate effects

1 _____

2 _____

3 _____

Long-term effects

4 _____

5 _____

D LISTEN FOR DETAILS Close your book. Watch the lecture again. Add details to your notes and correct any mistakes.

E CHECK YOUR UNDERSTANDING Use your notes. Choose the best answer, based on the lecture.

1 Sleep deprivation is defined as _____ hours of sleep each night.

    a needing more than ten
    b getting less than seven
    c getting seven to nine

2 _____ of adults suffer from sleep deprivation.

    a Ten percent
    b Forty percent
    c Sixty percent

3 A good night's sleep before a test helps students _____ .

    a remember new information
    b stay awake in class
    c finish the test faster

4 Doctors working 30-hour shifts were _____ more likely to make mistakes.

  a seven times
  b seventeen times
  c seventy times

5 Tired drivers cause _____ of car accidents in the United States.

  a 10 percent
  b 50 percent
  c 20 percent

6 Micro-sleep is defined as a person falling asleep _____ .

  a for several seconds
  b while driving
  c very quickly at night

7 People who get less sleep are more likely to _____ .

  a eat more
  b watch more movies
  c drink more coffee

8 Women who sleep less than five hours per night are 40 percent more

likely to _____ .

  a gain weight
  b fall into micro-sleep
  c have heart problems

9 We need more education about sleep deprivation because most people

_____ .

  a don't realize that it is dangerous
  b like staying up late
  c think they get enough sleep

HEAR the language

Signal Phrases

Speakers use **signal phrases** to make connections between ideas. Signal phrases can introduce an example (*for example* …), show cause and effect (*so* …), contrast ideas (*but* …), or emphasize a point (*in fact* …). A speaker may make a short pause after a signal phrase. Learning to recognize signal phrases will help you identify key ideas more easily.

> **EXAMPLES**
>
> *In fact,* *there are many serious consequences of not getting enough sleep.*
>
> *Recent studies show that 40 percent of adults get less than seven hours of sleep each night.* *So that means four out of ten adults are suffering from sleep deprivation.*

A LISTEN Listen and complete the statements from the lecture.

1. _____, if you get less than seven hours of sleep on most nights, you'll start suffering from sleep deprivation.

2. So, _____, anything to do with memory, making decisions, thinking—all of these are affected by the lack of sleep.

3. _____, at school. How many of you have stayed up all night to study for a big test?

4. _____, some studies have shown a connection between the amount of sleep students get and their grades in school.

5. _____ let's think about work.

6. _____ there are also long-term consequences of sleep deprivation, especially to our health.

7. _____, there's a link between lack of sleep and weight gain.

8. _____, people who get less sleep are more likely to get sick and to have serious health problems.

9. _____ they don't realize the cause.

10. _____ we need stronger health education programs to teach people about this problem.

B PAIR WORK Practice saying the sentences with a partner. Be sure to use a short pause after the signal phrase.

TALK about the topic

Paraphrasing

A FOLLOW THE DISCUSSION Watch as the students talk about sleep. Read each statement. Then check (√) who agrees with it. More than one student may agree.

Rob   Alana   Ayman   Molly

	Rob	Alana	Ayman	Molly
1 I have a question about the lecture.	☐	☐	☐	☐
2 I learned something new about sleep.	☐	☐	☐	☐

What are the students doing in their discussion of the lecture? Circle one or more.

a paraphrasing ideas   **b** giving relevant examples   **c** clarifying information

B LEARN THE STRATEGIES Watch the discussion again. Circle the phrases you hear. Then check (√) the discussion strategy that the student uses.

	Expressing an opinion	Paraphrasing
1 Alana: "Uh-huh. (I think / She said) seven to nine hours, so eight hours on average, right?"	☐	☐
2 Ayman: "So (that means / in my opinion,) it affects the public's health, in other words."	☐	☐
3 Ayman: "Oh, (good point / she said no)."	☐	☐
4 Molly: "This is really interesting (in other words / to me)."	☐	☐
5 Ayman: "(I believe / That means) sleep makes our memories stronger."	☐	☐

Discussion Strategy   When you **paraphrase**, you restate another person's idea in your own words. Here are some common ways of introducing paraphrased ideas: *What she meant was ... , In other words ... , His point was ... , She basically said ... .*

C TRY IT In a small group, discuss one or more of these topics. Try to use the discussion strategies.

- Based on your own experience, what are the effects of not getting enough sleep?
- What can people do to get more sleep at night?
- What can governments, schools, and employers do to help people get more sleep?

REVIEW your notes

REVIEW Read your notes. Did you write down key words and phrases? Can you explain the main ideas? Work with a partner to discuss and complete these notes.

def. of sleep deprivation: _____

_____

def. of micro-sleep: _____

_____

	Effects of sleep deprivation ...	Ex.
... on the brain		
... at school		
... at work		
... while driving		
... on health		

TIP!
Be sure you can explain the important ideas from the lecture.

🔊 **Now you are ready to take the Unit Test and the Proficiency Assessment.**

EXPRESS your ideas

Solving a Public Health Problem

In this unit, you have learned about one public health issue: the effects of sleep deprivation and the importance of a good night's sleep. What are some public health issues that you think are important?

TASK Give a short presentation about a public health issue that you think is important. Work with a partner to prepare and practice.

Prepare

1 Brainstorm. Look at the list of public health problems. Then add an idea.

Air pollution	Obesity (being overweight)
Dirty water	Smoking
Drug or alcohol addiction	Your idea: _____
Not enough exercise	

Presentation Strategy: Using signal phrases

To help your audience prepare for your presentation, use signal phrases to introduce your ideas. See p. 25 Focus Your Attention for a list of signal phrases.

2 Choose four problems and rank them three times. With a partner, discuss your rankings and why they are similar or different. Which do you think is the most important problem to solve?

Very harmful ↑	Affects a lot of people ↑	Difficult to solve ↑
1 _____	1 _____	1 _____
2 _____	2 _____	2 _____
3 _____	3 _____	3 _____
4 _____	4 _____	4 _____
↓ Not very harmful	↓ Affects a few people	↓ Not difficult to solve

3 Choose one public health issue from the list to talk about. Make an outline.

Practice

4 Practice with your partner. Practice using signal phrases to introduce your ideas.

5 Practice by yourself.

Present

6 Deliver your presentation to the class. Use signal phrases to introduce your ideas.

7 As you listen to your classmates' presentations: Note which health problems are most important to solve.

Evaluate

8 After all the presentations are finished, discuss the information, including: *What public health problems are most important? How can we start to solve the problems?*

9 Use the *Unit 3 Presentation Evaluation Form* (in Appendix C) to evaluate your classmates' presentations.

OUTLINE: SOLVING A PUBLIC HEALTH PROBLEM

I Introduction: Introduce the public health problem you will talk about

II Description of the health problem

Describe the problem and explain who is affected by it

Explain how difficult it is to solve the problem

Explain why we should try to solve it

III Conclusion: Suggest one way to solve the problem

IV Interaction: Answer questions from the audience

4 Negotiating for Success

CONNECT to the topic

A negotiation is a discussion between people who are trying to agree on something. Knowing how to negotiate well can help you solve problems with your friends, family, and classmates. Negotiation skills are also important for solving problems in business.

A THINK ABOUT IT We use different strategies to solve disagreements with different people. Look at the list of strategies. Check (√) the strategy you would use with each person. Compare answers with a partner.

Strategy	Parent	Brother / Sister	Friend	Teacher / Boss	Classmate / Coworker
• Do what the other person wants	☐	☐	☐	☐	☐
• Explain your side of the problem	☐	☐	☐	☐	☐
• Tell the other person why he or she is wrong	☐	☐	☐	☐	☐
• Ask questions to understand the other person's point of view	☐	☐	☐	☐	☐
• Get angry and yell	☐	☐	☐	☐	☐
• Get into a physical fight	☐	☐	☐	☐	☐
• Do nothing	☐	☐	☐	☐	☐
• Other: _____	☐	☐	☐	☐	☐

B TUNE IN Listen to an interview with Kristine Kinsella, an expert on negotiation. Then complete the sentences, based on the interview.

1 The goal of negotiation is to find a solution that _____ accept.

2 Kristine Kinsella gives an example of a negotiation between _____ .

3 They disagree about _____ .

4 One person wants _____ , and the other wants _____ .

C DISCUSS Discuss these questions in a small group: *What strategies are most effective for negotiating a solution to a problem? What strategies are not effective? Why?*

BUILD your vocabulary

A LISTEN The boldfaced words are from the unit lecture on negotiating. Listen to the sentences. Guess the meanings of the boldfaced words. Then match the words with their definitions.

_____ **1** I try to **avoid** having arguments with my coworkers. I change the topic or agree with the person so that we won't argue.

_____ **2** David has a different **approach**. His way of handling problems is to argue that his idea is right.

_____ **3** We need to get along because a comfortable work environment **benefits** everyone. People work better when they get along with each other.

    a prevent something from happening
    b be useful or helpful to someone
    c a way of dealing with a situation

_____ **4** My boss **blames** me because the project isn't finished. She says it's my fault.

_____ **5** I don't think she understands the **circumstances**. I need to tell her what happened to delay the project.

_____ **6** Before I talk to my boss, I want to **confer** with my coworker. I want to talk to her to see what she thinks I should do.

    d discuss something with someone before making a decision
    e think that someone is responsible for something bad
    f the facts or events surrounding a situation

_____ **7** David and I have a **conflict**. We don't agree on how to finish the work.

_____ **8** We are sewing blue jeans, and I'm worried that there isn't enough **fabric** to finish them.

_____ **9** David wants to use his own **technique** to finish the work. He thinks his way of doing it will work.

    g cloth
    h a disagreement
    i a particular way of doing something

$\longrightarrow$

_____ **10** Unfortunately, when I try to talk to him about it, he often **interrupts** me before I can finish what I'm saying.

_____ **11** I hope we can **resolve** this problem soon so we don't continue to have a problem.

_____ **12** We need to **concentrate** on getting the project done. We can't work on anything else until this is finished.

    j give all your attention or effort to something
    k find a solution to a problem
    l stop someone from talking by saying or doing something

B PAIR WORK Work with a partner. Notice the boldfaced words. Reorder the words and write the complete sentence. Take turns saying the sentences.

1 Different people take (business negotiations / **to** / **approaches** / different).

_____

2 When two people have different personalities, it is easy (for / **conflicts** / each other / to have / **with** / them).

_____

3 Understanding the personality of the other negotiator can help (**in** / the negotiation process / your **success** / to ensure).

_____

4 A good negotiator is almost always able (an **agreement** / the other person / **with** / to reach).

_____

5 Before finishing your negotiations with another company, it's important (**with** / your decision / about / your team members / to **confer**).

_____

6 My coworker is (**concerned** / making / **with** / mostly / a lot of money).

_____

7 I try to (doing / **on** / a good job / **concentrate**).

_____

8 I try to (my coworkers / keep / **with** / a good working **relationship**).

_____

9 I don't like to work late, but I (**to** / my boss / usually / **give in**) when she asks me to stay to finish something.

_____

10 My family **blames** (the long hours / **my boss** / that I spend at work / **for**).

_____

FOCUS your attention

Lists

Speakers often list items during a lecture. For example, a speaker may list the steps in a process.
Listen for lists so you can number and write steps or items in your notes.

PHRASES THAT INTRODUCE A LIST OR ITEMS IN A LIST	
There are (three) things ...	*There are (four) steps ...*
The first (thing) is ...	*First, ...*
The second (thing) is ...	*After ...*
	Now ...
	Finally, ...

A TRY IT **Listen to an excerpt from a business lecture. What ideas does the speaker list?
Complete the notes as you listen.**

Emotions in Negotiations

How to deal with feelings:

1)

2)

3)

B PAIR WORK **Compare notes with a partner.**

WATCH the lecture

A THINK ABOUT IT You are about to watch the unit lecture on business negotiation. What do you think is the most important goal of a successful negotiation?

a to keep a good relationship with other businesspeople

b to find the best solution for your business

c to find the best solution for everyone

d other: _____

Professor David Reed

B LISTEN FOR MAIN IDEAS Close your book. Watch the lecture and take notes.

C CHECK YOUR UNDERSTANDING Use your notes. Read each statement. Then correct the errors in the underlined phrases, based on the lecture. Write the correct answers.

1 The lecture describes <u>two approaches</u> to negotiation.

_____

2 In the "win-win" approach, a negotiator tries to reach a decision that <u>makes the other person happy</u>.

_____

3 A clothing company and a <u>clothing store</u> are the two sides in the professor's example.

_____

4 The first step in negotiation is to <u>explain your side of the problem</u>.

_____

5 The next step is to <u>argue for the solution that is best for your company</u>.

_____

D LISTEN FOR DETAILS Close your book. Watch the lecture again. Add details to your notes and correct any mistakes.

E CHECK YOUR UNDERSTANDING Use your notes. Match each action with the result discussed in the lecture.

ACTION

_b_ **1** If you learn to negotiate now, ...

____ **2** If you use a hard approach, ...

____ **3** If you use a soft approach, ...

____ **4** If you use a "win-win" approach, ...

____ **5** If you listen and don't interrupt the other person, ...

____ **6** If you blame the other person, ...

____ **7** If you explain your problem using "I" statements, ...

____ **8** If you discuss all the possible solutions, ...

RESULT

a you might agree to decisions that are bad for you.

b your business will benefit over time.

c you may hurt your relationship with the other person.

d you can keep a good working relationship with the other person.

e you may make the other person angry.

f you can find the best solution for both sides.

g you can avoid blaming the other person.

h you can hear the other person's side of the problem.

HEAR the language

Sentence Rhythm for Lists and Contrasting Points

Spoken English has a **rhythm** of stressed and unstressed words. Stressed words are emphasized by saying them louder, longer, and higher in pitch. Unstressed words are spoken more quickly and are often linked together.

Speakers often stress key words in a **list of points**. They also stress key words to **contrast two points**.

Learning to hear the stressed words will help you focus more easily on the speaker's important ideas.

> **EXAMPLE**
> *Fortunately, there are a **few** things you can do to deal with feelings in a negotiation. **One** thing you can do is to tell each other how you feel … The **second** thing is to listen …*

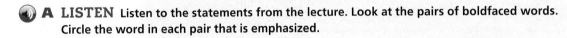 **A LISTEN** **Listen to the statements from the lecture. Look at the pairs of boldfaced words. Circle the word in each pair that is emphasized.**

Contrast Between Points

1 That's because many people perceive only **two approaches** to negotiation: the **hard approach** and the **soft approach**.

2 If you are a **hard negotiator**, you are concerned with "winning."

3 **Hard negotiators** will concentrate on, on getting the decision they want.

4 In the end, **hard negotiators** may get what they want.

5 So in contrast, **soft negotiators** are more concerned with avoiding conflict.

6 **This approach** to negotiation isn't good because **soft negotiators** often agree to decisions that are bad for them or bad for their business.

7 So instead of a **hard** or a **soft** approach, successful negotiators, like myself, take a win-win approach, where there isn't a **winner** or a **loser**.

List of Points

8 Well, there are **two important** techniques that will help you to do this.

9 The **first technique** is to listen and to understand.

10 The **second technique** is to work together to reach a solution.

B PAIR WORK **Practice saying the sentences with a partner. Be sure to emphasize the circled words.**

TALK about the topic

Expressing an Opinion

A FOLLOW THE DISCUSSION Watch as the students talk about different approaches to business negotiations. Read each opinion. Then check (✓) who agrees with it. More than one student may agree.

River   Hannah   Mia   Manny

	River	Hannah	Mia	Manny
1 I think the "win-win" approach to negotiations is best.	☐	☐	☐	☐
2 I like the "hard" approach.	☐	☐	☐	☐
3 There are a lot of "hard" businesspeople in the world.	☐	☐	☐	☐

What are the students doing in their discussion of the lecture? Circle one or more.

a defining the term *negotiate*   **b** giving relevant examples   **c** sharing opinions

B LEARN THE STRATEGIES Watch the discussion again. Complete the comments with the words you hear. Then check (✓) the discussion strategy that the student uses.

I can't say	I mean	I think	really	you like

	Asking for clarification or confirmation	Expressing an opinion
1 Hannah: "Well, yeah, I mean, _____ it's important that people listen to each other."	☐	☐
2 Manny: "Actually _____ that I agree with that."	☐	☐
3 Others: "Really?" " _____ ?" "No?"	☐	☐
4 Manny: "No, _____ , we're talking about business. The goal's to make money."	☐	☐
5 Hannah: "So _____ the hard approach?"	☐	☐

Discussion Strategy In academic settings, you have many opportunities to **express your opinions**— your thoughts, feelings, and positions. Start your opinions with expressions like *I think*, *I believe*, and *In my opinion*, but make sure to support them with facts, examples, and other forms of support!

C TRY IT In a small group, discuss one or more of these topics. Try to use the discussion strategies.

- Which approach to negotiation do you think is the best? Why? Do you think different techniques should be used in different situations? Give examples.
- Think about a time when you had a conflict and had to negotiate a solution. How did you solve the problem? Did you use any of the techniques explained in the lecture?

REVIEW your notes

REVIEW Work with a partner to discuss and complete your notes from the lecture.

	"Hard" approach	"Soft" approach	"Win-win" approach
Goal of approach			
Problems w / approach (if any)			

"Win-win" Approach Details

<u>2 main techniques:</u>

1. _____

   • when other per. is talking, DO: _____

   • when other per. is talking, DON'T: _____

2. _____

   • avoid blaming ea. other—how?: _____

Finding solution together—how?: _____

> **TIP!**
> Remember: You can organize a list of information by numbering the points.

🔊 **Now you are ready to take the Unit Test and the Proficiency Assessment.**

EXPRESS your ideas

My Experience with Negotiation

In this unit, you have learned about negotiation in business. Do you think that negotiation skills are important in business? Do you think they are important in your personal life?

TASK Give a short presentation about your experience with negotiation. Work with a partner to prepare and practice.

Prepare

1 Brainstorm. Think about a time that you had a conflict and had to use negotiation. Interview your partner, asking some of these questions:

- *Who was involved in the conflict? For example, a parent and child, teacher and student, boss and employee, two friends, or two businesses.*
- *What was the conflict about?*
- *What kind of negotiation did you use to resolve the conflict— hard, soft, win-win, or other? Was it successful?*

2 Make an outline.

Practice

3 Practice with your partner. Practice speaking slowly and looking at the audience.

4 Practice by yourself.

Present

5 Deliver your presentation to the class. Speak slowly and look at the audience.

6 As you listen to your classmates' presentations:

- Take notes on the main ideas of each presentation. Note which negotiation seemed most difficult.
- Write one question to ask each presenter.

Evaluate

7 After all of the presentations are finished, compare the stories and discuss the information, including: *Which negotiation was the most difficult? Why?*

8 Use the *Unit 4 Presentation Evaluation Form* (in Appendix C) to evaluate your classmates' presentations.

Presentation Strategy: Controlling speech speed

When you present, pay attention to how quickly you speak. Often, speakers get nervous and start to speak too quickly.

- Try to relax!
- Speak slowly (take a breath after each sentence!) and look at your audience to make sure they are following you.
- Pause after important ideas, to give the audience time to understand your point.

OUTLINE: MY EXPERIENCE WITH NEGOTIATION

I Introduction: Introduce the conflict and who was involved

II Your experience with the negotiation

Describe the approach you used to resolve the conflict (hard, soft, win-win, or other)

Explain the main points on both sides

Describe the final agreement

III Conclusion: Give your opinion about the negotiation: Was it a successful negotiation? Why or why not?

IV Interaction: Answer questions from the audience

5 Modern Art

CONNECT to the topic

Modern art is the name for art that was created in the recent past. There are many different kinds of modern art. The painting above is an example of modern art.

A THINK ABOUT IT Look at the painting above. Check (✓) the adjectives that describe the painting. Then add your own adjectives. Compare answers with a partner.

☐ beautiful   ☐ expensive   ☐ weird

☐ bold   ☐ happy   other: _____

☐ boring   ☐ interesting   _____

☐ colorful   ☐ natural   _____

☐ confusing   ☐ ugly   _____

B TUNE IN Listen to an interview with art historian Michiko Fujii, talking about the painter Kazuo Shiraga. Then choose the best answers, based on the interview.

1 The Gutai Group of artists was founded in Japan in _____ .

  a 1944   **b** 1954   **c** 1964

2 The Gutai Group used different materials and tried new _____ in their art.

  a techniques   **b** colors   **c** paints

3 Kazuo Shiraga swung his body from a rope and painted with _____ .

  a his feet   **b** his hands   **c** everyday items

4 Shiraga wanted to show _____ in his art.

  a strong feelings   **b** movement and action   **c** a new way of thinking

C DISCUSS Discuss these questions in a small group: *Do you like the painting above? Why or why not? What kind of art do you like?*

LEARNING OUTCOMES
In this unit you will:
- listen for phrases that signal a definition
- recognize main ideas from an art history lecture
- fact-check statements about an art history lecture
- identify and practice pausing between thought groups
- recognize and practice expressions of disagreement
- review and summarize your lecture notes to prepare for the unit test
- give a presentation about art, using visual aids

BUILD your vocabulary

A LISTEN The boldfaced words are from the unit lecture on abstract art. Listen to each description of a famous painter. Read along. Guess the meanings of the boldfaced words. Then match the words with their definitions.

Leonardo da Vinci (1452–1519) was an Italian inventor, painter, and sculptor. He also **created** many drawings of people, animals, plants, and **objects**, such as machines and weapons. One of his most famous works of art is the *Mona Lisa*, a painting of Lisa Gheradini, the wife of a successful Italian businessman. People like it because it is **realistic**. It shows exactly what she looked like. The painting is most famous for Mona Lisa's smile. From any **viewpoint**—standing in front of the painting or to the side—it looks like Mona Lisa is smiling at you.

Mona Lisa by Leonardo da Vinci

_____ 1 created   **a** made

_____ 2 objects   **b** a place from which you see something

_____ 3 realistic   **c** showing things as they are in real life

_____ 4 viewpoint   **d** things you can see or touch

Claude Monet (1840–1926) helped develop a new **style** of painting called Impressionism, which **emerged** in France in the late 1800s. Monet is famous for his outdoor scenes of lakes and the ocean. Other painters in this **category** included Pierre-Auguste Renoir, Edgar Degas, and Mary Cassatt. Impressionist painters didn't mix colors together. Instead, they made small dots of **pure** color.

Antibes by Claude Monet

_____ 5 style   **e** a group of people or things that are similar

_____ 6 emerged   **f** began to be known

_____ 7 category   **g** not mixed with anything else

_____ 8 pure   **h** the particular way something is done, created, or performed

Frida Kahlo (1907–1954) was a Mexican painter famous for her brightly colored paintings and **traditional** Mexican clothing. In many of her paintings, she **communicates** her feelings of pain and sadness. For example, in her painting *The Two Fridas*, Kahlo used the **image** of a bleeding heart to **represent** the sadness she felt over the end of her marriage.

The Two Fridas *by Frida Kahlo*

____ 9 **traditional**	**i**	express thoughts and feelings
____ 10 **communicate**	**j**	being done in a particular way for a long time
____ 11 **image**	**k**	show something
____ 12 **represent**	**l**	a picture of a person or thing

B PAIR WORK Work with a partner. Notice the boldfaced words. Circle the best word to complete each sentence. Take turns saying the sentences.

1 The *Mona Lisa* was **created** (by / to) da Vinci in the early 1500s.

2 The *Mona Lisa* is a (realistic / reality) **painting**.

3 You can look at the painting from (different / differently) **viewpoints**.

4 Monet's paintings fall in the **category** (of / to) Impressionist art.

5 Impressionist painting **emerged** (under / in) the 1800s.

6 Impressionist paintings had an important **influence** (in / on) other artists.

7 Impressionist artists **painted** (with / by) pure colors.

8 A bleeding heart **represents sadness** (in / to) Kahlo's painting.

9 In *The Two Fridas*, Kahlo shows two **images** (to / of) herself.

10 Shiraga used a different **style of** (paints / painting).

11 Shiraga's paintings communicate **the ideas** (to / of) action and movement.

12 Shiraga did not paint (traditional / tradition) **paintings**.

FOCUS your attention

Definitions

Speakers often give definitions in a lecture. Listen for definitions so that you can write them in your notes.

SIGNALING A DEFINITION

Speakers often emphasize the term they will define in the following ways:

- by pronouncing the term slowly and carefully
- by spelling the term
- by repeating the term
- by pausing
- by asking a rhetorical question

PHRASES THAT INTRODUCE A DEFINITION

What is modern art?

Modern art means ...

Modern art is ...

We say this is modern art because ...

Modern art isn't ... Instead, it's ...

How do we define the term modern art?

🔊 **A TRY IT** Listen to an excerpt from a lecture on art history. What definition does the speaker give? Complete the notes as you listen.

Art History

Portrait = picture of _____

- painting, _____, or sculpture → shows person's

  appearance

- all paintings w / people ≠ portraits

- focus on the _____

B PAIR WORK Compare notes with a partner.

WATCH the lecture

Professor Emma Gertz

A THINK ABOUT IT You are about to watch the unit lecture on abstract art. The three paintings on the next page will be discussed in the lecture. Using these two sentence starters, discuss the paintings with a partner.

- This is a painting of ...
- I like / don't like this painting because ...

B LISTEN FOR MAIN IDEAS Close your book. Watch the lecture and take notes.

C CHECK YOUR UNDERSTANDING Use your notes. Check (√) each term that describes the painting, based on lecture.

	Maria Picasso Lopez, the Artist's Mother	Portrait of Dora Maar	Contrasting Sounds
Portrait	√		
Representational	√		
Realistic			
Abstract			
Cubism			
Non-representational			
Pure abstraction			

Now match the terms with their definitions.

_____ **1** traditional art

_____ **2** representational abstract art

_____ **3** non-representational abstract art

      a doesn't show an image from the real world and isn't realistic
      b shows an image from the real world but isn't realistic
      c shows an image from the real world and is realistic

Picasso's Maria Picasso Lopez, the Artist's Mother

Picasso's Portrait of Dora Maar

Kandinsky's Contrasting Sounds

D LISTEN FOR DETAILS Close your book. Watch the lecture again. Add details to your notes and correct any mistakes.

E CHECK YOUR UNDERSTANDING Use your notes. Mark the statements *T* (true) or *F* (false) based on the lecture. Correct the false statements.

_____ 1 Modern art is art that was made during the 19th century.

_____ 2 Picasso painted the portrait of his mother when he was 50 years old.

_____ 3 In the early 1900s, many artists experimented with new types of art.

_____ 4 Picasso's *Portrait of Dora Maar* is an example of pure abstraction.

_____ 5 Cubism tried to show a person or object from different viewpoints.

_____ 6 Kandinsky painted his first abstract paintings in 1937.

_____ 7 Kandinsky used lines, shapes, and colors to represent the way people looked.

_____ 8 Kandinsky said that when he looked at a painting, he could hear music.

HEAR the language

Pausing Between Thought Groups

In spoken English, speakers separate groups of words—called "**thought groups**"—with short pauses. Pauses may separate thought groups, which are made of sentences, short phrases, or even single words. Pausing in speech is similar to punctuation in writing. It helps you understand and follow the speaker's meaning.

> **EXAMPLE**
> *But first / we need to define modern art / and understand / how it's different from / traditional art /*

A LISTEN Listen to the statements from the lecture. Notice when the speaker pauses between thought groups. Write a slash (/) when you hear a pause between a group of words. Note that punctuation indicating a pause has been removed.

1 Before 1900 most artists created what we call traditional art

2 Representational means that it represents something from the real world like a person an object or a scene in nature

3 In this painting Picasso depicts his mother using realistic details and colors including the color of her skin her brown hair and the white dress she was wearing

4 So many artists including Picasso wanted to create art that was new that was different from traditional art

5 So this is called representational abstract art

6 Now one goal of cubism was to show something from different viewpoints all at one time

7 Now the second category of abstract art is non-representational abstract art

8 In them he used lines shapes and colors to show his feelings

9 For example in this painting circles are meant to be peaceful shapes

10 But after Kandinsky died in 1944 his work continued to have a major influence on other abstract artists who followed him

B PAIR WORK Practice saying the sentences with a partner. Be sure to pause between groups of words.

TALK about the topic

Disagreeing

A FOLLOW THE DISCUSSION Watch as the students talk about abstract art. Read each opinion. Then check (√) who agrees with it. More than one student may agree.

May   Qiang   Yhinny   Michael

	May	Qiang	Yhinny	Michael
1 I like abstract art.	☐	☐	☐	☐
2 I like traditional art.	☐	☐	☐	☐
3 I don't understand abstract art.	☐	☐	☐	☐

What are the students doing in their discussion of the lecture? Circle one or more.

a reviewing the main points   **b** discussing examples   **c** sharing opinions

B LEARN THE STRATEGIES Watch the discussion again. Complete the comments with the words and phrases you hear. Then check (√) the discussion strategy that the student uses. More than one answer may be possible.

in my opinion	I respect your opinion	I'm like you	yeah	what do you guys think

	Agreeing	Asking for opinions or ideas	Disagreeing	Expressing an opinion
1 Michael: "Of all the art that we've talked about today, Kandinsky's is the best, _____ ."	☐	☐	☐	☐
2 Yhinny: "_____ , but, I mean, his style is sort of strange."	☐	☐	☐	☐
3 Qiang: "_____ . I'm a traditionalist."	☐	☐	☐	☐
4 Michael: " Well, _____ ? Like, OK, traditional is fine."	☐	☐	☐	☐
5 May: "Oh, _____ ."	☐	☐	☐	☐
6 May: "Is that strange?"	☐	☐	☐	☐

Discussion Strategy It is important to express **disagreement** without being rude. One way to do this is to first acknowledge the other person's point: *I see what you're saying, but …* Some people soften their disagreement with an apology: *I'm sorry, but … .* And body language and tone can also make your message more polite.

C TRY IT In a small group, discuss one or more of these topics. Try to use the discussion strategies.

- Which of the three paintings discussed in the lecture do you like most? Why?
- What type of art do you prefer—traditional art or modern art? Why?

Modern Art   **49**

REVIEW your notes

REVIEW Work with a partner to discuss the meanings of the following terms, using examples from the lecture. Then complete these notes.

Term	Def.	Ex.
traditional art	the style of art made before 1900	the portrait of Picasso's mother
modern art		
representational		
realistic		
abstract		
cubism		
non-representational		
pure abstraction		

> **TIP!**
> Be sure you can define the key words from the lecture.

🔊 **Now you are ready to take the Unit Test and the Proficiency Assessment.**

EXPRESS your ideas

Describing a Work of Art

In this unit, you have learned about different categories of art, including traditional art, modern art, and abstract art. You have learned about some famous artists and the styles of painting that they created. What artists or works of art do you like?

TASK Give a short presentation about a work of art in a style that you like. Work with a partner to prepare and practice.

Prepare

1 Brainstorm. Discuss these questions:

- *What is your favorite kind of art? Who is your favorite artist?*
- *What is the most memorable work of art you have ever seen? Why did you like it?*

2 Find a picture of an artwork by an artist not discussed in the lecture. Find some information about the artist and the artwork. Make an outline.

Practice

3 Practice with your partner or a group. Practice using your visual aid.

4 Practice by yourself.

Present

5 Deliver your presentation to the class. Use your visual.

6 Answer 2–3 questions from the audience.

7 As you listen to your classmates' presentations:

- Take notes on the main ideas of each presentation. Note which work of art you liked best.
- Write one question to ask each presenter.

Evaluate

8 After all of the presentations are finished, discuss the information, including: *Which is your favorite work of art? Why do you like it?*

9 Use the *Unit 5 Presentation Evaluation Form* (in Appendix C) to evaluate your classmates' presentations.

Presentation Strategy: Using visual aids

A visual aid is something to look at that helps explain the ideas in your presentation. A visual aid can be a picture, video, chart, or object that helps the audience see and understand the ideas you are talking about.

Tips

- Make your visual aid large and clear enough for everyone in the audience to see.

- Use visual aids that support the ideas in your presentation.

- Avoid writing too many words on your visual aid. Use only the words you need to label your pictures or to state main points. Make sure your writing is correct and easy to read.

- Stand next to your visual so that everyone in your audience can see it. Point to the visual, but continue to make eye contact with the audience when you are speaking. Do not turn your back to the audience.

- Use phrases to describe details in your visual:

Here, you can see / there is / there are ...	*At the bottom ...*
This is / These are ...	*In the middle ...*
At the top ...	*In the upper right-hand / lower left-hand corner ...*

OUTLINE: DESCRIBING A WORK OF ART

I Introduction: Introduce the name of the artwork, the artist, and the year it was created

II Description of the artwork

Tell the style of the artwork and how it was made

Describe what you can see in the art

Explain what the art communicates or represents

III Conclusion: Summarize why you like this work of art

6 Robots

CONNECT to the topic

A robot is a machine that can move by itself. The Czech writer Karel Capek introduced the word *robot* in 1921. The word comes from the Czech word *robota*, which means "forced labor." Today, scientists in the field of robotics develop robots to do many different kinds of work.

A THINK ABOUT IT Work in a group of four. What types of work can robots do? What *can't* robots do? Why? Make a list of jobs. Compare answers with a partner.

Robots can do the work of ...   Robots cannot do the work of ...

_____   _____

_____   _____

_____   _____

_____   _____

B TUNE IN Listen to an interview with Daniela Karpov, an expert on robots. Then check (√) the statements as *True* or *False*. Correct the incorrect information.

	True	False
1 Fifty percent of all jobs will be replaced by robots or machines.	☐	☐
2 In most jobs, machines can do about 30 percent of the work.	☐	☐
3 A robot can prepare food quickly.	☐	☐
4 Robots are good at understanding people's feelings.	☐	☐

C DISCUSS Discuss these questions in a small group: *How do you feel about the increasing number of robots? What are the benefits? What are the dangers? What kind of robot would you like to have?*

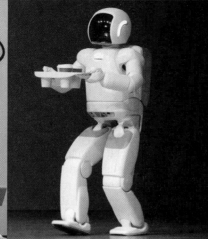

BUILD your vocabulary

 A LISTEN The boldfaced words are from the unit lecture on robots. Listen to each passage. Read along. Guess the meanings of the boldfaced words. Then match the words with their definitions.

If you are looking for a career in a growing field, you should consider studying robotics, and have the opportunity to work on robots like these:

Drones are flying robots. Some drones are controlled by a person, while other drones fly **automatically**, controlled by a computer. Computer-controlled drones are **programmed** to fly to a specific place and complete a **task**, such as watching weather conditions, or sending video of forest fires. These aircraft have also been used to **explore** hard-to-reach places, like the tops of mountains.

Drones are also available for **personal** use. There is a growing **industry** of companies that build and sell drones directly to the public.

_____ 1 **automatically**	**a**	an activity to be completed
_____ 2 **programmed**	**b**	belonging to one particular person
_____ 3 **task**	**c**	a group of businesses that produces a particular type of thing
_____ 4 **explore**	**d**	instructed by a computer to do something
_____ 5 **personal**	**e**	find out about a place by traveling through it
_____ 6 **industry**	**f**	without a person making it work

Nanorobots are extremely small robots—smaller than a human cell. Nanorobots may someday be used in medicine. For example, doctors may put nanorobots inside patients' bodies, and **utilize** them to **obtain** information and find early signs of disease. Nanorobots may also be used to treat cancer, instead of **surgery** or other treatments. Just like a human doctor uses the **senses** of sight and touch to find disease in the body, these tiny **mechanical** disease fighters have "senses" to help them find cancer cells. Then they attach themselves to the cancer cells and release medicine to kill the cancer. As you can see, robotics is not a **dull** field of study—there are many new and exciting uses for robots in the future!

____ 7 **utilize**		**g** a medical treatment in which a doctor cuts open your body
____ 8 **obtain**		**h** involving a machine
____ 9 **surgery**		**i** not interesting or exciting
____ 10 **senses**		**j** the powers of sight, hearing, feeling, taste, and smell
____ 11 **mechanical**		**k** get something
____ 12 **dull**		**l** use something for a particular purpose

B PAIR WORK Work in pairs. Student A: Read aloud sentence starters 1–5 from Column 1. Student B: Listen and complete each sentence with a phrase from Column 2. Notice the boldfaced words. Switch roles for 6–10.

COLUMN 1	COLUMN 2
1 Drones can be **controlled**	**a about** a person's health.
2 We use our **sense**	**b by** a person or a computer.
3 I'd like to **get a drone**	**c for** my own personal use.
4 The automobile industry **uses robots**	**d in** car factories.
5 Doctors must **obtain information**	**e of** sight to see the things around us.
6 Nanorobots will be **utilized**	**f for** cancer inside a person's body.
7 Doctors **perform surgery**	**g in** medicine.
8 Nanorobots may **look**	**h on** their patients.
9 A robot can **pick**	**i to** fly automatically.
10 Drones are **programmed**	**j up** heavy objects.

FOCUS your attention

Examples and Restatement

Speakers explain general ideas by giving examples and by restating ideas in a different way.

PHRASES THAT INTRODUCE AN EXAMPLE
For example …
For instance …

PHRASES THAT INTRODUCE A RESTATEMENT
In other words …
That is …

A TRY IT Listen to an excerpt from a lecture on robotics. Complete the notes as you listen. Notice that *e.g.* is short for "example."

Education

≠ teachers

Robotics competitions

    All ages   e.g. Junior FIRST LEGO League -_____ yrs old

    Specific task   e.g. move on _____

                        aerial = _____

  Motivate students = build _____ → excited – math & _____

B PAIR WORK Compare notes with a partner.

WATCH the lecture

A THINK ABOUT IT You are about to watch the unit lecture on robots. What do you know about robots? Discuss these questions with a partner:

1 What makes robots different from other types of machines?

2 How are robots used today? Where are they used?

Professor Nancy Lee

B LISTEN FOR MAIN IDEAS Close your book. Watch the lecture and take notes. Pay attention to the introduction to help you focus on the main ideas and organize your notes.

C CHECK YOUR UNDERSTANDING Use your notes. Number the ideas from 1 to 9 in the order discussed in the lecture.

Robots ...

_____ **a** can do dull work.

_____ **b** are becoming popular for personal use.

_____ **c** are used to explore places where people can't go.

_____ **d** must perform a task.

_____ **e** replace parts on people's bodies.

_____ **f** can do dirty or dangerous work.

_____ **g** are used as medical assistants.

_____ **h** obtain information from the environment.

_____ **i** are controlled by computers.

D LISTEN FOR DETAILS Close your book. Watch the lecture again. Add details to your notes and correct any mistakes.

E CHECK YOUR UNDERSTANDING Use your notes to complete the statements, based on the lecture.

1 Robots need at least one _____ .

    a eye
    b sense
    c wheel

2 A Gasbot robot can smell gas leaks, and a biosensor robot can _____ .

    a feel earthquakes
    b hear sound
    c taste food

3 A robot in a food processing plant might _____ .

    a look for a dirty surface to clean
    b smell food to make sure it's fresh
    c taste food for quality

4 A robot in a chocolate factory can perform the same task _____ times per day.

    a 200
    b 2,000
    c 20,000

5 The police and military use robots to do work that is too _____ for people.

    a complicated
    b dangerous
    c tiring

6 Small robots are used to explore inside volcanoes and _____ .

    a in large forests
    b on other planets
    c under the ocean

7 One type of medical robot can _____ .

    a look at sick patients
    b heal broken bones
    c perform surgery

8 Robotic hands can be _____ a person's body and _____ the person's mind.

    a removed from – attached to
    b controlled by – sent to
    c attached to – controlled by

9 Some people now have personal robots that are _____ .

    a spouses
    b pets
    c teachers

10 People worry that robots in the future will _____ .

    a become less expensive
    b learn to copy themselves
    c start to control us

HEAR the language

Contractions

Contractions are often used in spoken English. A contraction is a combination of two words shortened into one word. Learning to understand contractions will help you understand spoken English better.

COMMON CONTRACTIONS

BE verb	*I am = I'm*	*you are = you're*	*it is = it's*
WILL	*I will = I'll*	*you will = you'll*	
NOT	*cannot = can't*	*is not = isn't*	*do not = don't*

EXAMPLE

*To answer this, **we'll** look at examples of where robots are used today and the tasks that **they're** performing.*

A LISTEN Listen to the statements from the lecture. Circle the form you hear.

1 But first, (I would / I'd) like to review a basic definition of "robot."

2 So, robots are programmable: (They are / They're) controlled by computers.

3 For example, researchers in Mexico developed "Gasbot" robots to detect gas leaks that humans (cannot / can't) smell.

4 In other words, robots do work that people (cannot / can't) do, because (it is / it's) too dangerous or difficult—or (do not / don't) want to do, because (it is / it's) dirty or dull.

5 (It is / It's) impossible for a person to do a task like this as efficiently as a robot.

6 Robots also perform work (that is / that's) too dirty or too dangerous for humans.

7 Robots can explore volcanoes where (it is / it's) very hot.

8 People obviously (cannot / can't) go into a volcano!

9 (I will / I'll) leave you with that thought.

10 Next time, (we will / we'll) talk more about the benefits and dangers of living with robots.

B PAIR WORK Practice saying the sentences with a partner. Be sure to use contractions.

TALK about the topic

Trying to Reach a Consensus

A FOLLOW THE DISCUSSION Watch as the students talk about the lecture on robots. Read each opinion. Then check (√) who agrees with it. More than one student may agree.

Kenzie   Hugh   Shelley   Ben

	Kenzie	Hugh	Shelley	Ben
1 It's interesting that robots have "senses."	☐	☐	☐	☐
2 Using robots for surgery is a great idea.	☐	☐	☐	☐
3 Robots shouldn't replace humans.	☐	☐	☐	☐

What are the students doing in their discussion of the lecture? Circle one or more.

a giving relevant examples   **b** sharing opinions   **c** defining the term *robots*

B LEARN THE STRATEGIES Watch the discussion again. Complete the comments with the words and phrases you hear. Then check (√) the discussion strategy that the student uses. More than one answer may be possible.

do we all agree	maybe we can	I wrote that	right	like it can

	Offering a fact or example	Trying to reach a consensus
1 Shelley: "Well, there are different kinds of robots, _____?"	☐	☐
2 Ben: "Like, it has to be controlled by a computer. _____?"	☐	☐
3 Hugh: "A robot must have at least one 'sense'—you know, _____ touch or see or hear."	☐	☐
4 Shelley: "_____ robots have to do a job, like, pick up a part and connect it to something."	☐	☐
5 Kenzie: "Hey guys, _____ stop for now?"	☐	☐

Discussion Strategy Getting a group to **reach a consensus**, or agree, can be challenging. One approach is to use questions to identify areas of agreement (*So, when is everyone free to meet again?*). You can then make suggestions based on how people answered your question (*Sounds like Sunday is open for everyone—does that work?*).

C TRY IT In a small group, discuss one or more of these topics. Try to use the discussion strategies.

- Would you like to have a personal robot? If so, what would you like it to do?
- What do you think about using robots to perform tasks such as caring for sick people?
- How can robots make our lives better? What dangers could robots create?

REVIEW your notes

REVIEW Work with a partner to discuss and complete these notes. Use your notes from the lecture.

Robots

def. - robot
- machine
- controlled by computer
- must do 2 things:

    1. _____
      – see, feel, hear, smell, taste

    2. _____

- Gasbot: smells gas
- biosensor: _____
- automotive: _____
- food processing: _____

"4 Ds"
dull / _____ / dirty / _____
Ppl can't / don't want to do

Uses	Examples
Industry	Chocolate factory - pick up 20K times / day
Police / Military	
Exploration	
Medical assistants	
Robotic body parts	
Personal use	

TIP!
Remember: Use the abbreviation *e.g.* or *ex.* to show an example.

 Now you are ready to take the Unit Test and the Proficiency Assessment.

EXPRESS your ideas

A Robot for You

In this unit, you have learned about different types of robots. What kind of robots would you like to have?

TASK Give a short persuasive presentation about one type of robot. Try to "sell" your robot to the audience. Work with a partner to prepare and practice.

Note: At the end of the presentations, members of the audience will decide how much they like the robot by giving it a score from 1 to 5. In your presentation, you must convince the audience to give your robot the highest score. The presenter with the best score wins.

How much do you like the robot?

1 = Not interested.

2 = It's OK.

3 = I like it.

4 = I really like it.

5 = I must have it!

Presentation Strategy: Showing enthusiasm

Showing enthusiasm means speaking with excitement and energy. Showing enthusiasm helps the audience feel more interested in your presentation.

You can show enthusiasm with:

- facial expressions: Smile and use eye contact to show you are interested and excited about your topic.

- voice: Speak strongly and confidently. Use stress and intonation to emphasize the key words in your presentation.

- word choice: Use details to clearly explain your topic. Use descriptive adjectives and adverbs to show why it is interesting (*incredibly useful, extremely useful, the most useful*).

Prepare

1 Brainstorm. Think of a robot that you think is valuable and useful. It can be a type of robot discussed in this unit, a robot you have found through research, or an idea for a robot that you invent. Try to find a picture of the robot, or draw a picture.

2 Answer these questions about the robot:

- *What does the robot look like?*

- *What tasks does it perform?*

- *Where is it usually used (in industry, at home, in the military, etc.)?*

- *Why should your audience choose to support this robot?*

3 Make an outline.

Practice

4 Practice with your partner. Practice showing enthusiasm. Give each other feedback.

5 Practice by yourself.

Present

6 Deliver your presentation to the class. Show enthusiasm for your robot.

7 As you listen to your classmates' presentations:

- Take notes on the main ideas of each presentation. Note which robot you liked best.

- Write one question to ask each presenter.

Evaluate

8 After all the presentations are finished, discuss the information, including: *What were the most useful robots? What were the most interesting robots?* Count the scores for each robot. The robot with the most points wins.

9 Use the *Unit 6 Presentation Evaluation Form* (in Appendix C) to evaluate your classmates' presentations.

OUTLINE: A ROBOT FOR YOU

I Introduction

Introduce the robot (name, where it is made, type of robot)

Describe the robot: what it looks like, the senses it has, the tasks it can perform, and where it is used

II Reasons your robot is the best

Explain one way your robot is interesting or useful, include supporting details

Explain a second way your robot is interesting or useful, with supporting details

III Conclusion

Give a final thought about why your robot is the best

Ask the audience to give your robot a score (1 to 5 points)

IV Interaction: Answer questions from the audience

7 Interactive Games

CONNECT to the topic

Media are different ways that we communicate. Traditional media include *print* media (books, magazines, newspapers), radio, television, and movies. New media include a variety of *digital* media, such as email, blogs, and Internet websites. One popular type of media is interactive games—computer games, video games, and mobile games played on smartphones and tablets.

A THINK ABOUT IT Read the list of media-related activities. What are your favorite activities? Number the activities in order from 1 (most favorite) to 7 (least favorite). Compare answers with a partner.

_____ reading books, magazines, newspapers

_____ watching movies or television

_____ listening to the radio

_____ listening to music

_____ reading online blogs or Internet sites

_____ using online social media

_____ playing interactive games

B TUNE IN Listen to the interview with Lisa Goodwin, an interactive game developer. Then choose the best answers, based on the interview.

1 Worldwide, people spend about _____ dollars on games every year.

  a 150 million   **b** 100 billion   **c** 10 billion

2 The average gamer in the United States is _____ years old.

  a under 18   **b** 25   **c** 35

3 About 40 percent of gamers play _____ games.

  a mobile   **b** social   **c** computer

4 The two most popular games are _____ games.

  a action and shooting   **b** sports and role-playing   **c** word and puzzle

C DISCUSS Discuss these questions in a small group: *Do you play interactive games? Why or why not? What are the benefits of playing interactive games? What are the problems?*

BUILD your vocabulary

A LISTEN The boldfaced words are from the unit lecture on interactive games. Listen to the sentences. Guess the meanings of the boldfaced words. Then match the words with their definitions.

_____ **1** One goal of game designers is to create games that are **engaging**. When players are interested in the game, they want to keep playing.

_____ **2** I failed a test yesterday, and now I'm feeling **depressed**. I need to do something to lift my spirits!

_____ **3** Researchers are interested in learning the **potential** effects of gaming on social skills. They want to find out if playing games might have an effect on our personal relationships.

    a sad
    b interesting
    c possible

_____ **4** _3-D Monster Maze_ was one of the first **three-dimensional** computer games. The designer of the game wanted players to feel like they are inside of a maze trying to find their way out.

_____ **5** _Call of Duty_ is a **violent** war game. The goal of the game is to shoot and kill enemy soldiers.

_____ **6** _The Legend of Zelda_ is a popular **fantasy** game. The player travels through an imaginary world while playing the game.

    d something produced by the imagination
    e having or seeming to have length, width, and depth
    f using force to hurt or kill someone

_____ **7** I love to play _League of Legends_. Sometimes I get so **involved** in playing, I completely forget about the time.

_____ **8** Sometimes my game playing **interferes** with my schoolwork. I play games when I should be studying or doing my homework.

_____ **9** Media experts research the effects of game playing on people's **cognitive** abilities. They study the impact of gaming on our ability to think and learn.

    g connected to thinking
    h stop or slow something
    i actively participating in something

$\longrightarrow$

_____ **10** One **concern** about games is that they teach bad behavior. For example, in _Grand Theft Auto_, players are criminals who fight others to get ahead in the game.

_____ **11** Will playing games with fighting and shooting lead to **aggressive** behavior in real life? Will the players want to hurt others in their daily life?

_____ **12** If you spend a lot of time playing games and don't want to stop playing, you may have an **addiction**.

    j a strong and harmful need to have or do something
    k worry
    l ready to fight or argue

B PAIR WORK Work with a partner. Notice the boldfaced words. Reorder the words and rewrite the sentences. Take turns saying the sentences.

1 Experts are (the kind of media / **concerned** / **about** / children use).

_____

2 Some researchers look at the (media / of / kids' development / **on** / **effects**).

_____

3 They study the (**relationship** / Internet use / **between** / success in school / and).

_____

4 We need to (about / **drawbacks** / spending time online / **of** / think / the).

_____

5 Spending too much time alone on the computer can (children's social development / **interfere** / **with**).

_____

6 Most experts agree that children should be (activities / with other children / **in** / **involved**).

_____

7 Studies show there is a (**connection** / social activities / **between** / and children's health).

_____

8 Playing sports can lead to (children's physical health / **in** / **improvement**).

_____

9 Another (is psychological health / playing sports / **benefit** / **of**). Active children are less anxious and depressed.

_____

FOCUS your attention

Evidence and Support

Speakers often provide research or *evidence* to support their ideas. Evidence is information that shows your ideas are true. One type of evidence is studies or surveys done by researchers to find out new information.

PHRASES THAT INTRODUCE RESEARCH OR EVIDENCE	
To talk about one study	**To summarize several studies**
One study / survey looked at …	*Research shows … / Studies show …*
The researchers studied …	*It is estimated that …*
The study / survey found that …	*Researchers believe …*
According to this study / survey …	

A TRY IT Listen to an excerpt from a lecture on educational games. What research or evidence does the speaker mention? Complete the notes as you listen.

Educational Games

Recent Study:

- ~ _____ students bet. 6-8

- 3 groups:

     1 played an ed. game

     2 "   "   game w / _____

     3 mixed game playing w / _____ activities

Results: Grp.# _____ showed most improvement

     Remembered _____ information

     → Teachers should combine games & classroom activities

B PAIR WORK Compare notes with a partner.

WATCH the lecture

Professor Julian Young

A THINK ABOUT IT You are about to watch the unit lecture on the advantages (positive effects or potential benefits) and drawbacks (negative effects or potential problems) of playing interactive games. What do you think are some advantages and drawbacks of interactive games?

Interactive games are good because ...

• _____

• _____

Interactive games are bad because ...

• _____

• _____

B LISTEN FOR MAIN IDEAS Close your book. Watch the lecture and take notes.

C CHECK YOUR UNDERSTANDING Use your notes. Complete the outline with the effects of gaming discussed in the lecture. Write the letters of the effects in the order they're discussed in the lecture. Two of the effects are not mentioned.

Potential Benefits

____ 1

____ 2

Potential Problems

____ 3

____ 4

Effects of Gaming

a motivation

b spatial ability

c aggressive behavior

d not getting enough exercise

e problem-solving ability

f game addiction

D LISTEN FOR DETAILS Close your book. Watch the lecture again. Add details to your notes and correct any mistakes.

E CHECK YOUR UNDERSTANDING Use your notes to decide if the statements are T (true) or F (false), based on the lecture. Correct the false statements.

_____ **1** Spatial ability is the ability to understand the relationship between objects in space.

_____ **2** One study found that playing three-dimensional puzzle games improved participants' spatial abilities.

_____ **3** Failing in games causes players to feel frustration and want to quit.

_____ **4** Playing games interferes with students' motivation to work on difficult tasks.

_____ **5** Gaming becomes an addiction when game playing interferes with a person's relationships and personal goals.

_____ **6** A sign of game addiction is when players prefer the fantasy world of games to spending time with real people.

_____ **7** One study found that 13- and 14-year-olds who play violent games are more likely to argue with their parents and get into fights.

_____ **8** Studies clearly show that playing violent games causes aggressive behavior.

HEAR the language

Sentence Rhythm That Signals Important Ideas

Spoken English has a **rhythm** of stressed and unstressed words. Stressed words are emphasized by saying them louder, longer, and higher in pitch. Unstressed words are spoken more quickly and are often linked together. When a word is stressed, the most emphasis is put on the stressed syllable in the word. Learning to hear the stressed words will help you focus more easily on the speaker's important ideas.

> **EXAMPLE**
> *And remember / by "media" / we mean different ways that we communicate / including traditional media / such as newspapers / television / and movies /*

A LISTEN Listen to the statements and questions from the lecture. Look at the thought groups separated by a slash (/). Underline one word in each thought group that receives the most stress.

1 It'll come as no surprise / that video games / have been one of the fastest growing types / of new media

2 Spatial ability / is the ability / to understand / the relationship between / objects in space

3 The study found / that players did much better / on the spatial ability test / after playing the game

4 Instead / players feel excitement / and want to try again / and again

5 Teachers / can employ game psychology / to keep students working / on difficult learning tasks

6 But / gaming becomes an addiction / when it starts to interfere / with a person's relationships

7 Another sign / is the person feels angry / or anxious / or depressed / when they are not able to play

8 Does playing / a violent game / make someone want to hurt another person / in real life

9 These studies / only show a connection / between violent games / and aggressive behavior

10 Well, there's something / for us all to think about / the potential benefits / and drawbacks / of the increased use / of interactive games / in our society

B PAIR WORK Practice saying the sentences with a partner. Be sure to stress the underlined words.

TALK about the topic

Asking for Clarification or Confirmation

A FOLLOW THE DISCUSSION Watch the students talk about the lecture on interactive games. Read each opinion. Then check (√) who agrees with it. More than one student may agree.

Hugh   Shelley   Ben   Kenzie

	Hugh	Shelley	Ben	Kenzie
1 Interactive games help with spatial ability.	☐	☐	☐	☐
2 Parents shouldn't let their kids play violent games.	☐	☐	☐	☐
3 Violent games don't necessarily cause violent behavior.	☐	☐	☐	☐

What are the students doing in their discussion of the lecture? Circle one or more.

a clarifying information   **b** giving relevant examples   **c** defining the term *interactive games*

B LEARN THE STRATEGIES Watch the discussion again. Complete the comments with the phrases you hear. Then check (√) the discussion strategy that the student uses.

are you sure	said it was	I have it here	say that again	should or shouldn't

	Asking for clarification or confirmation	Paraphrasing
1 Shelley: "Wait. _____? *Aren't* bad for you?"	☐	☐
2 Hugh: "_____ in my notes—wait … here: There are some potential benefits of interactive games."	☐	☐
3 Kenzie: "And personally, I don't think parents should let their kids play violent games." **Hugh:** "_____?"	☐	☐
4 Ben: "But it's not necessarily cause and effect, remember?" **Hugh:** "Wait, wait. Can you _____?"	☐	☐
5 Shelley: "Yeah. The way the professor _____ maybe some kids are *already* aggressive."	☐	☐

Discussion Strategy To **clarify** means to make something clearer. To **confirm** is to remove doubt. You can clarify or confirm by restating what you understood (*You mean …*) or by asking *Do you mean … ?* Or you can ask open-ended questions like *What do you mean?* and *Could you clarify … ?*

C TRY IT In a small group, discuss one or more of these topics. Try to use the discussion strategies.

- Do you think there are benefits to playing interactive games?
- Do you think interactive games are bad for children? Why or why not?
- Do you play interactive games? If so, which games do you like to play? What do you like about them?

REVIEW your notes

REVIEW Read your notes. Did you write down key words and their meanings? Can you explain the main ideas of the lecture? Work with a partner to discuss and complete these notes.

Effects of Interactive games

Potential benefits:	What research shows:
Potential problems:	

TIP!
A chart is one way you can organize the positive and negative sides of an issue. The positives can go in one row, and the negatives can go in another row, for easy comparison.

Now you are ready to take the Unit Test and the Proficiency Assessment.

EXPRESS your ideas

Media Survey Results

In this unit, you have learned about different types of media and the positive and negative effects of playing interactive games. Do you feel advances in media have made your own life better?

TASK Give a short group presentation about media use. Work in a group of 3 or 4 to prepare, practice, and present.

Prepare

1 Brainstorm. Look at the list of activities related to media use and choose a topic to present about:

> Downloading music
> Going to the movies
> Playing educational games
> Playing interactive games
> Using apps to study English
>
> Using cell phones in public / class
> Using social media
> Sharing photos online
> Your idea: _____

2 Write three questions to ask in a survey about people's use of the media. Example questions:

- *How often do you … ?*
- *What's your favorite type of … ?*
- *What are some problems with … ?*
- *How does _____ affect you?*

3 Survey others outside of your group, or outside your class. Each group member should interview at least four different people. Note information about each person you survey, such as the person's age, gender, and nationality.

4 Share your results and combine your data. What did you learn about people's media use? Make an outline, and assign one part to each person in the group.

Practice

5 Practice with your group. Practice making transitions between each speaker.

6 Practice your section by yourself.

Present

7 Deliver your presentation to the class. Take turns speaking and make transitions between speakers.

8 As you listen to your classmates' presentations note the differences in results.

Evaluate

9 After all of the presentations are finished, discuss the information, including: *How were each group's survey results similar or different? Which results were the most surprising to you?*

10 Use the *Unit 7 Presentation Evaluation Form* (in Appendix C) to evaluate your classmates' presentations.

Presentation Strategy: Giving a group presentation

In a group presentation, it's important that you work together as a team to prepare and deliver your presentation.

Tips for Giving Group Presentations:

- Work together to plan the content, create visual aids, and practice your presentation.

- Divide your presentation into equal parts so that each group member can speak equally.

- Practice your presentation together so you can time the length and give each other feedback.

- Use transitions between each speaker: *Next, Maria will discuss … , Now, Ted will talk about … .*

- Stand together as a group to answer questions at the end. Take turns answering questions.

OUTLINE: MEDIA SURVEY RESULTS

I Introduction: Introduce your group, your topic, and say why you chose this topic (1 person)

II Your survey questions and results (1–3 people)

> Introduce your first survey question and explain the results
>
> Introduce your second survey question and explain the results
>
> Introduce your third survey question and explain the results

III Conclusion: Explain what your survey results show (1 person)

IV Interaction: Answer questions from the audience (everyone in your group)

8 Genetically Modified Food

CONNECT to the topic

Genetically modified food (also called GM food) is a new type of food. It comes from plants that have been changed in the laboratory. Scientists change the genes inside the plants to make them grow in a different way. A gene is a small part of a cell. It controls the qualities that a parent passes on to its offspring.

A THINK ABOUT IT Complete this survey about genetically modified food. Check (✓) your opinion. Then compare answers in a small group.

	Strongly disagree	Disagree	Agree	Strongly agree
• We shouldn't change the genes of plants and animals.	☐	☐	☐	☐
• I only eat food that is grown without chemicals.	☐	☐	☐	☐
• I don't care what I eat, as long as it tastes good.	☐	☐	☐	☐
• I want to know where my food comes from.	☐	☐	☐	☐
• Scientific research can create healthier food.	☐	☐	☐	☐
• When I shop for food, I care most about low cost.	☐	☐	☐	☐
• I would eat genetically modified food.	☐	☐	☐	☐

B TUNE IN Listen to the interview with Ben Ramanna, an expert in genetically modified food. Then choose the best answers, based on the interview.

1 An example of genetically modified food is rice with a gene from _____ .

    a a corn plant   **b** a flower   **c** an insect

2 Some people want _____ genetically modified foods in stores.

    a labels on   **b** lower prices for   **c** laws against

3 _____ countries do not allow GM food to be grown or sold.

    a Some   **b** Many   **c** Most

C DISCUSS Discuss these questions in a small group: *Do you worry about where your food comes from, or whether it is genetically modified? Why or why not? What do you do to make sure you are eating healthy food?*

LEARNING OUTCOMES
In this unit you will:

- listen for key terms
- recognize main ideas from a biology lecture
- fact-check statements about a biology lecture
- identify and practice linking unstressed words
- recognize and practice changing the topic
- review with a partner to prepare for the unit test
- give a presentation comparing and contrasting two types of food

BUILD your vocabulary

A LISTEN The boldfaced words are from the unit lecture on GM food. Listen to the sentences. Guess the meanings of the boldfaced words. Then match the words with their definitions.

_____ **1** *E. coli* **bacteria** are very dangerous. If food has these bacteria on it, people can become very sick or die.

_____ **2** Doctors say we should **consume** eight glasses of water each day, including the water in the food we eat and in the things we drink.

_____ **3** Farmers grow **crops** such as wheat and corn.

   a plants that are grown for food
   b very small living things that sometimes cause disease
   c eat or drink

_____ **4** Most strawberry plants grow in warm places. However, scientists want to **modify** strawberry plants so they can live in cold weather.

_____ **5** The weather this year was **normal**. We had the usual amount of rain and snow.

_____ **6** I used a **pesticide** to kill the ants in my kitchen.

   d usual and expected
   e make small changes to something
   f a poisonous chemical used to kill insects

_____ **7** When the apples are ready to eat, the farmer **picks** them from the tree.

_____ **8** The corn grown in the United States is used **primarily** for feeding animals. Most corn is fed to cows, pigs, and chickens, not people.

_____ **9** We **purchase** most of our vegetables from local farmers, not a supermarket.

   g pull a fruit or vegetable from a plant
   h buy
   i mainly

_____ **10** I put the carrots in the refrigerator so they **retain** their freshness. If I don't, they get soft and don't taste good.

_____ **11** Oceans are one **source** of fish. Fish farms, lakes, and rivers are others.

_____ **12** My mother gave us **vitamins** every day. We took vitamin A for healthy eyes and vitamin D for strong bones.

j a place where you get something
k keep or hold on to
l a part of food that helps with good health

B PAIR WORK Work with a partner. Circle the best word to complete each sentence. Take turns saying the sentences.

1 (Genetically / Gene) **modified** food is made in the laboratory.

2 Scientists (modify / modifying) **genes** to make plants grow differently.

3 Scientists want to (solve / solved) **problems**.

4 E. coli are (common / commonly) **bacteria**.

5 **Just** (picked / picking) **fruit** is delicious.

6 Corn (stays / staying) **fresh** in the refrigerator.

7 Some people are against the (use / used) **of pesticides** to kill insects.

8 Our corn crop was (consumed / consumer) **by insects**.

9 Farmers (grow / grown) **crops** to sell.

10 Vegetables are a good (source / sources) **of vitamins**.

11 I didn't feel like shopping; I quickly (made / make) **a purchase** and then left the store.

12 Tomatoes don't **retain their** (flavor / flavored) after you pick them.

FOCUS your attention

Key Terms

Speakers often introduce important new terms in a lecture. They may explain how the term is pronounced or spelled. Listen for new terms so that you can write them down in your notes.

A TRY IT Listen to an excerpt from a lecture on biology. What key terms does the speaker introduce? Complete the notes as you listen.

Biology

Today: _____

– change genes inside living thing

– plant / animal grows differently

Also called: _____

B PAIR WORK Compare notes with a partner.

WATCH the lecture

A THINK ABOUT IT You are about to watch the unit lecture on genetically modified food. Based on what you've heard about GM food, what do you think the speaker's opinion will be? Circle your answer.

   a GM food is dangerous.

   b GM food can help people live better lives.

   c GM food is difficult to create.

Professor Simon Gato

 B LISTEN FOR MAIN IDEAS Close your book. Watch the lecture and take notes.

C CHECK YOUR UNDERSTANDING Use your notes. Match the type of food with the reason it was developed, based on the lecture. One reason is not mentioned in the lecture.

Food

_____ **1** FlavrSavr Tomato was developed to …

_____ **2** Bt Corn was developed to …

_____ **3** Golden Rice was developed to …

Reason

a grow better.
b cost less.
c solve a health problem.
d stay fresh longer.

 D LISTEN FOR DETAILS Close your book. Watch the lecture again. Add details to your notes and correct any mistakes.

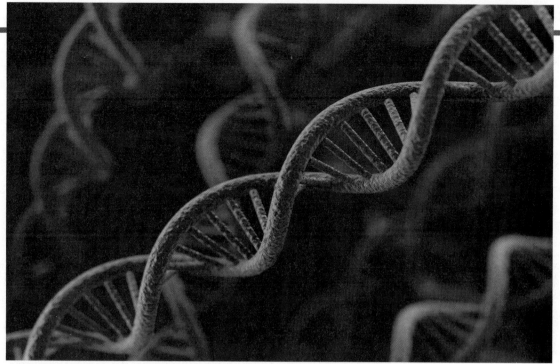

Genes are part of what is called our DNA, shown here. DNA is inside every cell of all living things.

E CHECK YOUR UNDERSTANDING Use your notes to decide if the statements are *T* (true) or *F* (false), based on the lecture.

1 The FlavrSavr Tomato ...

_____ has a gene that stops the tomato from changing color.

_____ was the first genetically modified food sold in US supermarkets.

_____ was popular because shoppers thought it was healthier.

_____ is sold in supermarkets today.

2 Bt Corn ...

_____ is used instead of pesticides.

_____ kills insects but doesn't hurt people or animals.

_____ has a gene that comes from another plant.

_____ is used by farmers all over the world.

3 Golden Rice ...

_____ helps people who eat too much fat.

_____ could stop death and blindness in millions of children.

_____ has a vitamin A gene from a flower.

_____ is being studied to make it less expensive.

HEAR the language

Linking Unstressed Words

Spoken English has a rhythm of stressed and unstressed words. Stressed words are emphasized by saying the word louder, longer, and higher. **Unstressed words** are spoken more quickly and are often **linked** together: The final consonant from one word "jumps" to the next word. Learning to hear linked sounds will help you better understand "fast speech."

LINKING

Linked words	Spelling	Sounds like
A word ends with a consonant (sound) and the next word starts with a vowel (sound):	*has it*	*ha_sit*
	think about	*thin_kabout*
	made of	*ma_dof*
A word ends with and the next word begins with the same sound:	*has some*	*ha_some*
	think carefully	*thin_carefully*
	made daily	*ma_daily*

EXAMPLE

Now, doe_severyone remember our definition? (The /z/ sound in *does* jumps to the next word.)

A LISTEN Listen and complete the statements from the lecture with two or three linked words.

1 Genetic modification is when we change the genes _____ a living thing to make it grow in a different way.

2 Scientists have _____ to create all kinds of new plants, and it's really a very exciting time in this field.

3 Now _____ actually because it was the first genetically modified food to be

_____ US supermarkets, _____ 1994.

4 _____ RNA gene stops the chemical that makes tomatoes get soft.

5 And corn farmers have problems _____ called a rootworm.

6 _____ time, the only method for getting rid of these insects was the use of pesticides.

7 Now for farmers, Bt Corn is _____ the most popular genetically modified crops today.

8 They don't get enough food with vitamin A—you know, the _____ orange foods like carrots and sweet potatoes.

9 Over a million children die each year from a _____ vitamin A.

10 To make Golden Rice, scientists took a vitamin A gene from a plant—a daffodil,

_____ a flower.

B PAIR WORK Practice saying the sentences with a partner. Be sure to connect the sounds of the linked words.

TALK about the topic

Changing the Topic

A FOLLOW THE DISCUSSION Watch as the students talk about genetically modified food. Read each opinion. Then check (√) who agrees with it. More than one student may agree.

May   Qiang   Yhinny   Michael

	May	Qiang	Yhinny	Michael
1 I don't trust GM food.	☐	☐	☐	☐
2 I support GM food.	☐	☐	☐	☐
3 I think that big business wants to make money from GM food.	☐	☐	☐	☐

What are the students doing in their discussion of the lecture? Circle one or more.

a sharing opinions   **b** giving relevant examples   **c** clarifying information

B LEARN THE STRATEGIES Watch the discussion again. Complete the comments with the words and phrases you hear. Then check (√) the discussion strategy that the student uses.

agree to disagree	agreed	I agree	isn't that	let's talk about	no problem

	Agreeing	Changing the topic	Trying to reach a consensus
1 Qiang: "I mean, look at Bt Corn—it takes away the need for pesticides. _____ a good thing?"	☐	☐	☐
2 Yhinny: "Overall, _____ with Qiang."	☐	☐	☐
3 Michael: "OK. Maybe we should just '_____' on this one?"	☐	☐	☐
4 Others: "Sure." "_____." "Fine! _____!"	☐	☐	☐
5 Qiang: "_____ something else."	☐	☐	☐

Discussion Strategy In a discussion you may need to stop talking about one topic and talk about something else. By **changing the topic**, you can be sure to get all of your tasks completed. Use phrases such as *Let's move on ...* and *So how about we discuss _____ now.*

C TRY IT In a small group, discuss one or more of these topics. Try to use the discussion strategies.

- Do you think genetically modified food is safe to eat? Why or why not?
- Should governments allow genetically modified food to be grown? Why or why not?
- What other health or environmental problems could be solved by creating new genetically modified crops? Give an example.

REVIEW your notes

REVIEW Work with a partner to discuss and complete these notes. Use your notes from the lecture.

Genetic modification def.:

	FlavrSavr Tomato	Bt Corn	Golden Rice
Why developed?			
How modified?			
What modification does:			
# of people using today:			
Other:			

TIP!
A fun way to review the main points of a lecture is to compare notes with a classmate. You'll not only improve your notes, but you'll also get a better understanding of the lecture.

Now you are ready to take the Unit Test and the Proficiency Assessment.

EXPRESS your ideas

Comparing Two Foods

In this unit, you have learned about different kinds of genetically modified food. Some people think GM foods are good to eat, while other people think non-GM foods are better. What kind of food do you like or dislike?

TASK Give a short presentation comparing two types of food. Work with a partner to prepare and practice.

Prepare

1 Brainstorm. Look at the list comparing two types of food. In each pair, which one do you think is better? Why?

> Convenience food (microwave pizza, instant noodles) / Food made from scratch (from basic ingredients)
>
> Fried food / Low-fat food
>
> GM food / Non-GM food
>
> Organic food (grown without pesticide) / Non-organic food
>
> Restaurant food / Homemade food
>
> Spicy (hot) food / Mild food
>
> Sweet flavors / Savory (salty or spicy) flavors
>
> Vegetarian food / Food made with meat

Presentation Strategy: Comparing and contrasting

There are three ways that speakers can show contrasts (how two points are different):

	Examples
1) Use a <u>word or phrase</u> to contrast two points.	*On ONE hand, GM food can resist INSECTS. On the OTHER hand, it is sometimes more EXPENSIVE.*
2) Put extra STRESS on the words you are contrasting.	*ORGANIC foods are grown WITHOUT chemicals, but NON-organic foods are grown WITH chemicals.*
3) Gesture with one hand on one point and with the other hand on the contrasting point. (See photo at top of page.)	*Some people LIKE spicy food. However, OTHER people HATE it.*

---

2 Choose a pair of foods to compare. Make a chart listing the positive and negative aspects of each food. Think about aspects including taste, cost, health, and convenience.

3 Make an outline.

Practice

4 Practice with your partner. Practice contrasting points using phrases, word stress, and gestures.

5 Practice by yourself.

Present

6 Deliver your presentation to the class. Contrast your points using phrases of contrast, word stress, and gestures.

7 As you listen to your classmates' presentations:

- Take notes on the main ideas of each presentation. Note which presenters you agreed or disagreed with.

- Write one question to ask each presenter.

Evaluate

8 After all the presentations are finished, discuss the information, including: *Which presenters did you agree with? Which presenters did you disagree with? Why?*

9 Use the *Unit 8 Presentation Evaluation Form* (in Appendix C) to evaluate your classmates' presentations.

OUTLINE: COMPARING TWO FOODS

I Introduction: Introduce the types of food you are comparing

II Your opinion about the foods

Explain your opinion about food #1 with supporting reasons and examples

Explain your opinion about food #2 with supporting reasons and examples

III Conclusion: Explain which food you like better and why

IV Interaction: Answer questions from the audience

9 Design Thinking

CONNECT to the topic

Design is the process of planning how to create something new—what materials to use, how to put it together, and what it can do. There are many different areas of design, including *architecture* (the design of houses and buildings), *fashion design* (the design of clothing and shoes), *user interface design* (the design of websites, computer software, and apps), and *industrial design* (the design of consumer products made in factories). Design Thinking is a process used to create solutions to design problems.

A THINK ABOUT IT Look at the pictures of telephones over the years. How did the phones change from one design to the next? What do you think caused the changes? Compare answers with a partner.

Changes in ...

- Shape _____

- Size _____

- Material _____

- Technology _____

- Other _____

B TUNE IN Listen to an interview with Marc Latham, who answers the question "What do designers do?" Then choose the best answers, based on the interview.

1 Designers turn ideas into _____ .

   a physical things   **b** interesting questions   **c** popular products

2 Designers focus on _____ .

   a how much a product will cost   **b** how simple an idea is   **c** how a design will look and work

3 Good design _____ .

   a creates a lot of sales   **b** is usually expensive   **c** meets the needs of the user

C DISCUSS Discuss these questions in a small group: *Think of a product or item that is an example of "good design." What makes it a good design? Think of another product or item that is not well designed. What are the problems with it?*

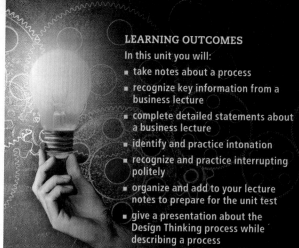

BUILD your vocabulary

A LISTEN The boldfaced words are from the unit lecture on Design Thinking. Listen to each passage. Read along. Guess the meanings of the boldfaced words. Then match the words with their definitions.

The Apple iPad, released in 2010, was an **innovative** new product that changed the market for tablet computers. However, development was not easy and the designers faced many challenges when they **implemented** the ideas for the design. They had to **focus** on technical issues, such as software development and battery life, as well as the look and feel of the new tablet. **Participants** on the design team worked long hours for many months to create the final design.

_____ 1 innovative

_____ 2 implemented

_____ 3 focus

_____ 4 participants

a give attention to something

b made changes according to a plan

c new and better

d people taking part in an activity

The design team created many different **prototypes** to see how the iPad looked and to test how well it worked. During this **phase** of the process, the designers tried different designs and **identified** problems with the prototypes. Early prototypes were large and heavy, so they **revised** the design to make the tablet thinner and lighter.

_____ 5 prototypes

_____ 6 phase

_____ 7 identified

_____ 8 revised

e a stage of development

f changed to make corrections and improvements

g discovered

h models used to test a design

The designers had a user-**centered** design process, trying to create a tablet that was easy to use without any instructions. Apple hoped that the iPad could be used by a **diverse** market—from businesspeople to artists. An especially large potential market was education. This meant that the tablet had to be simple for inexperienced users—children and **teens** who had never used a tablet before. Today, the story of the development of the iPad is used as a **case study** to teach designers about a successful design process.

____	**9** -centered	**i**	focused on a particular person or group
____	**10 diverse**	**j**	people between 13 and 19 years old
____	**11 teens**	**k**	a detailed examination of a process or situation over time
____	**12 case study**	**l**	very different from each other

B PAIR WORK Work with a partner. Student A: Read aloud sentences 1–6 in Column 1. Student B: Cover Column 1. Listen and complete the sentences in Column 2. Notice the boldfaced words. Switch roles for 7–12.

COLUMN 1	COLUMN 2
1 The design team has a **diverse group of** designers.	1 The design team has a **diverse group** _____ designers.
2 The goal is to **think of** innovative ideas.	2 The goal is to **think** _____ innovative ideas.
3 They are **focused on** creating a great design.	3 They are **focused** _____ creating a great design.
4 They made **prototypes of** the new design.	4 They made **prototypes** _____ the new design.
5 This is an important **phase of** the design process.	5 This is an important **phase** _____ the design process.
6 **Participants in** the design process work very long hours.	6 **Participants** _____ the design process work very long hours.
7 They wanted to **make a product for** children and teens.	7 They wanted to **make a product** _____ children and teens.
8 They **tested the product with** users.	8 They **tested the product** _____ users.
9 They **asked users about** their experience.	9 They **asked users** _____ their experience.
10 They **gathered data about** the problem.	10 They **gathered data** _____ the problem.
11 They **found a solution for** the problem.	11 They **found a solution** _____ the problem.
12 They **revised the design by** making it smaller.	12 They **revised the design** _____ making it smaller.

FOCUS your attention

Description of a Process

When speakers describe a process, they explain the phases in which something is done. Listen for expressions that introduce the different phases in a process. Also listen for an explanation of what happens in each phase.

PHRASES THAT INTRODUCE A PHASE

The first phase of the … process is to …
This second phase is …
The final phase is …

PHRASES THAT EXPLAIN WHAT HAPPENED DURING A PHASE

In this phase …
During this phase …
The goal of this phase is to …

A TRY IT Listen to an excerpt from a lecture on Design Thinking introducing a case study. What is the process for understanding a case study? Complete the notes.

> Case Studies
>
> Phases
>
> 1 _____ story
>
>   - _____
>
>   - timeline
>
> 2 _____ key issues
>
>   - actions / decisions
>
>   - _____ / not
>
> 3 _____ other possible actions
>
>   - mistakes
>
>   - do _____

B PAIR WORK Compare notes with a partner.

WATCH the lecture

Professor Helena Sonin

A THINK ABOUT IT You are about to watch the unit lecture featuring a case study in Design Thinking. The case study is about a design problem for a store at a shopping mall. Who would you want to help solve a design problem at a shopping mall? Why? Choose at least three people. Explain your choices to a partner.

architect   salesclerk

fashion designer   customer

store owner   other: _____

B LISTEN FOR MAIN IDEAS Close your book. Watch the lecture and take notes.

C CHECK YOUR UNDERSTANDING Use your notes. Write the descriptions for each phase of the Design Thinking process, based on the lecture. Two descriptions are not used.

Build a model	Include many different points of view	Test the design with real customers	Visit stores owned by other companies
Collect information	Observe customers	Think of as many ideas as possible	
Hold a "Grand Opening" party for customers			

Design Thinking Process: Phases

1 Understand _____

_____

2 Brainstorm _____

_____

3 Prototype _____

_____

D LISTEN FOR DETAILS Close your book. Watch the lecture again. Add details to your notes and correct any mistakes.

E CHECK YOUR UNDERSTANDING Use your notes. Complete the sentences, based on the lecture.

1 The Design Thinking case study is about a _____ called Sunflower.
  a children's clothing store
  b women's and teens' clothing store
  c women's shoe store

2 Sunflower had a problem with _____ their juniors department.
  a customers stealing from
  b finding good employees for
  c low sales in

3 The Design Thinking team asked customers questions about _____ .

   a how much money they planned to spend
   b the type of clothing they liked
   c their shopping experience

4 In addition to talking to customers, the Design Thinking team also talked to

_____ .

   a employees who worked for the store in the past
   b people who didn't go in the store
   c salespeople at other stores

5 Most teenagers did not know about Sunflower's _____ .

   a fashion website
   b juniors clothing section
   c weekly sales on juniors clothing

6 After the _____ phase, the design question was revised.

   a Understand
   b Brainstorm
   c Prototype

7 The Brainstorming team included store employees and _____ .

   a fashion designers
   b high school students
   c the owner of the company

8 The new design focused on making the juniors department _____ the
rest of the store.

   a have lower prices than
   b look different from
   c seem bigger than

9 The new design included places for girls to _____ .

   a buy a snack while shopping
   b sit down and talk with friends
   c take pictures of themselves

10 The prototype design of the store was tested for _____ .

   a three days
   b three weeks
   c three months

HEAR the language

Intonation for Finished and Unfinished Thoughts

As we saw in Unit 2, English speech has a pattern of **rising and falling intonation**. Intonation is the pitch (high and low) of the voice. The pitch can rise slightly (go up) or fall (go down). One use of intonation is to signal whether or not an idea is finished. Rising intonation shows that the speaker is not finished and plans to say more. Falling intonation shows that a speaker has completed an idea. Learning to notice intonation in sentences will help you become a better listener.

> **EXAMPLES**
>
> Unfinished: *Design Thinking is a way to identify problems ...*
>
> Finished: *Design Thinking is a way to identify problems and find solutions.*

A LISTEN Listen to the statements from the lecture. Listen for falling or rising intonation at the end. Check (√) if the statement is finished or unfinished.

	Finished (Falling intonation)	Unfinished (Rising intonation)
1 Sunflower has stores in a dozen large shopping malls around the country	☐	☐
2 The owners of Sunflower had tried to solve the problem by lowering the prices	☐	☐
3 *Human-centered* means understanding the experience of the users	☐	☐
4 We watched customers as they came in the store, observed where they went	☐	☐
5 So clearly, the store wasn't attracting teen customers	☐	☐
6 This second phase is the Brainstorm Phase	☐	☐
7 No judgment—just say your idea	☐	☐
8 It had bean bag chairs, an espresso bar, and a fridge stocked with juice	☐	☐
9 Well, we wanted the participants to relax	☐	☐
10 Specifically, we used splashy fun colors in the juniors section	☐	☐

B PAIR WORK Practice saying the sentences with a partner. Be sure to use the correct intonation for the finished and unfinished statements.

TALK about the topic

Interrupting Politely

A FOLLOW THE DISCUSSION Watch the students talk about Design Thinking. Read each opinion. Then check (√) who agrees with it. More than one student may agree.

Ben   Kenzie   Hugh   Shelley

	Ben	Kenzie	Hugh	Shelley
1 I like the idea of a human-centered process.	☐	☐	☐	☐
2 The brainstorm phase seemed like fun.	☐	☐	☐	☐
3 Having a diverse team was very important.	☐	☐	☐	☐

What are the students doing in their discussion of the lecture? Circle one or more.

a sharing opinions   **b** giving relevant examples   **c** reviewing important ideas

B LEARN THE STRATEGIES Watch the discussion again. Complete the comments with the words and phrases you hear. Check (√) the discussion strategy that the student uses. More than one answer may be possible.

good point	make a point	sorry	wow	add

	Agreeing	Expressing an opinion	Interrupting politely
1 Ben: "_____ . This case study has some great examples of innovation."	☐	☐	☐
2 Hugh: "Can I _____ here? Can I _____ something?"	☐	☐	☐
3 Hugh: "_____ , what I mean is … the important thing is the team was diverse."	☐	☐	☐
4 Ben: "_____ , Hugh. Having a diverse team was really important."	☐	☐	☐

Discussion Strategy You may need to **interrupt politely** in order to participate in an online discussion. One approach is to use body language to show you want to speak, such as making eye contact with the person talking, leaning forward, or gesturing with your hand. Another approach is to say something, such as *May I add something?, Can I make a point?*, or *Sorry, but I think … .*

C TRY IT In a small group, discuss one or more of these topics. Try to use the discussion strategies.

- When you have to solve a problem, how do you solve it? Have you ever used brainstorming or prototyping?
- What types of problems are best solved with Design Thinking? What problems would be difficult to solve that way?
- What are the advantages of using a diverse team of people to solve a problem? What are the disadvantages?

REVIEW your notes

REVIEW Read your notes. Did you write down key words and their meanings? Can you explain the main ideas of the lecture? Work with a partner to discuss and complete these notes.

Design Problem:	Case Study: Sunflower clothing store
	Jrs sales = not good
	Tried lower prices, diff brand, ads
	Q: How do we _____?

Phase 1: Understand	Gather data:
	human-centered = _____
	- observed / talked to _____ & _____
	Data:
	72% _____ 28% _____
	teens thought _____
	Revise Q: How do we _____?

Phase 2: Brainstorm	Think of many ideas — strange, crazy OK
	_____ team
	- customers - _____ → _____ ideas
	- employees
	Relaxing room
	1 great idea - make jrs dept _____
	- Jrs dept → _____

Phase 3: Prototype	Build _____
	- test w/ _____
	- _____
	3 wks — _____
	- sold _____

Design Solution:	Implemented in all 12 stores
	→ _____

> **TIPS!**
> Listen for two things in the description of a process:
> - the story of what happened during each phase
> - an explanation of the results of each phase

 Now you are ready to take the Unit Test and the Proficiency Assessment.

EXPRESS your ideas

Our Design Thinking Experience

In this unit, you have learned about the Design Thinking process. How would you solve a design problem?

TASK Give a short group presentation about solving a design problem using the Design Thinking process. Work with a group to prepare, practice, and present.

Prepare

1 Form a design team of 3 or 4 people. Try to create a diverse team with people who have different points of view. Give your team a name.

2 Use the Design Thinking process to solve a design problem.

3 Reflect on the experience. What went well? What was difficult? How happy are you with your design?

4 Make an outline, and assign one part to each person in the group.

> **Presentation Strategy: Describing a process**
> - Introduce the number of phases in the process: *There are (three) phases in the process …*
> - Introduce each phase: *We started with the first phase … , Then we began the next phase … , Then we moved on to the final phase …*
> - Describe what happened in each phase: *In this phase, we … ; The goal of this phase was … ; During this phase, we …*
> - Use other sequencing expressions to show the order of events within a phase: *First, … , Next, … , After that, … , Finally, …*

Understand Phase

a Think of a common activity that the group feels should be improved. Use a real activity that everyone in your group has experienced.
- Shopping at _____
- Riding the _____ (bus or train line)
- Doing _____ (a kind of activity) in our classroom

b Ask your classmates and people outside your class about the activity. Take notes on what they think works well, and what causes problems. As a team, discuss the results.

c Write your design question: How can we improve _____ (the activity)?

Brainstorm Phase

a With your team, brainstorm ideas to solve the design problem.

b Look at all the ideas, and identify the best solutions to the design problem.

Prototype Phase

Create a prototype of your design by making a drawing, map, or model. Show that your solution will work.

Practice

5 Practice with your group. Practice describing the steps in your group's Design Thinking process.

6 Practice your section by yourself.

Present

7 Describe the steps in your group's Design Thinking process.

8 As you listen to your classmates' presentations note the best solution to a design problem.

Evaluate

9 After all of the presentations are finished, discuss the information, including: *How were the Design Thinking processes similar or different? Which group came up with the best solution to their design problem?*

10 Use the *Unit 9 Presentation Evaluation Form* (in Appendix C) to evaluate your classmates' presentations.

> **OUTLINE: OUR DESIGN THINKING EXPERIENCE**
>
> I Introduction: Introduce your design team and explain your design question (1 person)
>
> II Your Design Thinking process (1–2 people)
>
>   Explain the data you found from your research
>
>   Describe the possible solutions brainstormed by the group
>
> III Conclusion: Show the prototype and explain your group's solution (1 person)
>
> IV Interaction: Answer audience questions (whole group)

10 Shackleton

CONNECT to the topic

In the early 1900s, explorers wanted to learn all they possibly could about the world. In 1914, explorer Sir Ernest Shackleton began planning a journey to Antarctica. He hired 28 men to go on the journey. In addition to the sailors who operated the ship, he also hired a photographer, an artist, four scientists, two doctors, and two engineers.

A THINK ABOUT IT Imagine that you have to pick people to go on Shackleton's trip to Antarctica. What qualities would those people need for a successful trip? Check (√) your top five qualities from the list or add your own. Share your answers with a partner.

☐ bravery

☐ physical strength

☐ intelligence

☐ education

☐ good communication skills

☐ ability to work well with others

☐ experience on a ship

☐ knowledge of Antarctica

_____

_____

B TUNE IN Listen to an interview with historian Paul Smith, talking about polar exploration. Then choose the best answers, based on the interview.

1 In the 1500s, explorers wanted to travel _____ .

   a to the North Pole   **b** to Antarctica   **c** between Europe and Asia

2 In the late 1700s, ships started traveling to Antarctica to search for

_____ .

   a the South Pole   **b** seals and whales   **c** a shorter way to Asia

3 Explorers landed on the continent of Antarctica in _____ .

   a the early 1800s   **b** the late 1800s   **c** the early 1900s

4 Antarctica is the coldest and _____ continent on Earth.

   a largest   **b** windiest   **c** oldest

C DISCUSS Discuss these questions in a small group: *Why do you think people want to explore far-away places like Antarctica or outer space? Would you like to be an explorer? Why or why not?*

BUILD your vocabulary

A LISTEN The boldfaced words are from the unit lecture on Sir Ernest Shackleton. Listen to each sentence. Then circle the best meaning of the boldfaced word.

1 In 1913, explorer Vihjalmur Stefansson led a trip on the ship the *Karluck* to the North Pole. He had a **crew** of thirteen sailors, ten scientists, and eight other people.

    a people who work on a ship   **b** people who travel by ship

2 The *Karluck* **sailed** north toward the Arctic Circle.

    a traveled over land   **b** traveled over water while pushed by wind

3 Soon, the ship became **stuck** in the ice and didn't move for three weeks. The ice floated slowly north, taking the ship with it.

    a unable to stop   **b** unable to move

4 Stefansson did not care about his crew or treat them with **respect**. Instead of staying with them, he took five men and left the ship. He never returned to get the crew.

    a concern and thoughtfulness   **b** anger and rudeness

5 However, ship's officer Bob Bartlett took care of the crew even though it wasn't his job. This showed **leadership**.

    a being a leader   **b** following a leader

6 Bartlett **ordered** the crew off the ship and onto the ice. Everyone did what he said.

    a told someone to do something   **b** asked someone to do something

7 The ship was finally **crushed** by the ice, breaking it into many pieces.

    a made a big hole in something   **b** pressed so hard that something breaks

8 The ship **sank** under the water.

    a turned on one side   **b** went below the water

9 The crew **survived** on the ice by catching birds and other animals to eat.

    a continued to live   **b** continued to travel

10 Bartlett tried to keep the crew's **morale** up, but they were depressed and fearful.

    a belief about right and wrong   **b** level of positive feelings

11 With the goal of getting help, Bartlett took a small **team** of men and left.

    a a group of people who dislike each other   **b** a group of people who work together

12 Meanwhile, another ship **rescued** the crew in September 1914.

    a saved   **b** left

13 During the eight months they lived on the ice, 11 people died. However, the crew **credited** Bartlett with trying to save them.

    a believed he made a mistake   **b** believed he did something good

14 Today, Bartlett is remembered as a hero for being **loyal** to the crew, while Stefansson is remembered for leaving his men to die on the ice.

    a always supporting other people   **b** thinking only of oneself

B **PAIR WORK** Work in pairs. Student A: Read aloud sentence starters 1–7 from Column 1. Student B: Listen and complete each sentence with a phrase from Column 2. Notice the boldfaced words. Switch roles for 8–14.

COLUMN 1	COLUMN 2
1 Stefansson began an **exploration**	**a** **in** the ice.
2 Stefansson didn't **treat the crew**	**b** **the order to** leave the boat.
3 Stefansson didn't **interact** well	**c** **signs of** poor leadership.
4 The ship became **stuck**	**d** **of** the North Pole.
5 By leaving the ship, Stefansson **showed**	**e** **under** the water.
6 Bartlett **gave**	**f** **with respect**.
7 The ice crushed the ship, and it **sank**	**g** **with** his men.
8 Bartlett tried to **keep**	**h** **together** as a team.
9 The men **worked**	**i** **by** a boat.
10 The men **survived**	**j** **up** the crew's morale.
11 The crew was **loyal**	**k** **to** Bartlett.
12 The men were **rescued**	**l** **as a hero** for rescuing the men.
13 Bartlett was **credited**	**m** **by** staying positive.
14 Bartlett is **remembered**	**n** **with** saving the crew.

FOCUS your attention

Numbers, Dates, and Periods of Time

Speakers often use numbers. It's important to understand the numbers in order to write them down correctly. Understanding syllable stress can help you hear the difference between similar numbers:

- Numbers ending in -teen have stress on the second syllable: 13 = thirTEEN.
- Numbers ending in -ty have stress on the first syllable: 30 = THIRty.

When speakers discuss events in history, they often describe the events in *chronological* (time) order. Listen for the dates and periods of time. In speech, dates are usually expressed with ordinal numbers such as *first, tenth,* and *thirtieth.* When you take notes, abbreviate the dates by writing them as numbers. Notice the following abbreviations: ~ = about; < = less than; > = more than.

What you hear:	How it's written:
DATES	
on October second, nineteen fourteen	10 / 2 / 1914 (US) or 2 / 10 / 1914
in January nineteen fifteen	1 / 1915
in nineteen sixteen	1916
PERIODS OF TIME	
for ten months	10 mos.
for nearly five days	~ 5 days
less than a week	< 1 wk.
more than / over three hours	> 3 hrs.

A TRY IT Listen to an excerpt from a history lecture. Complete the notes as you listen.

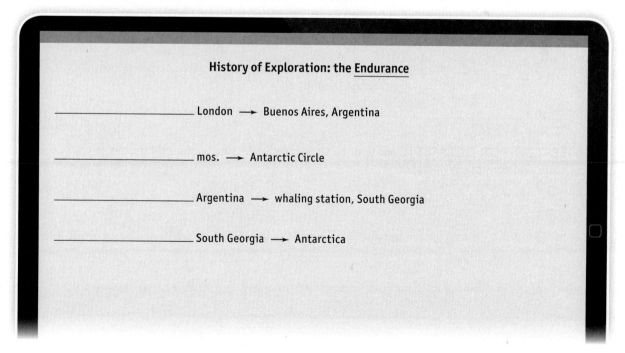

History of Exploration: the Endurance

_____ London ⟶ Buenos Aires, Argentina

_____ mos. ⟶ Antarctic Circle

_____ Argentina ⟶ whaling station, South Georgia

_____ South Georgia ⟶ Antarctica

B PAIR WORK Compare notes with a partner.

WATCH the lecture

Professor Zachary Boyd

A THINK ABOUT IT You are about to watch the unit lecture on Shackleton and his ship, the *Endurance*. Look at the map of the journey of the *Endurance* on the following page. Think about these questions.

1 How long do you think the trip lasted?

2 Why do you think people remember the trip today?

B LISTEN FOR MAIN IDEAS Close your book. Watch the lecture and take notes.

C CHECK YOUR UNDERSTANDING Complete the timeline with dates and times, using the map and your lecture notes.

Date / Time

1 _____ The *Endurance* left England.

Ⓐ 2 _____ The *Endurance* entered the Antarctic Circle and became stuck in the ice.

3 _____ = months until spring begins.

Ⓑ 4 _____ = Shackleton ordered the crew off the ship.

5 _____ = The *Endurance* sank.

6 _____ = The ice began to melt.

Ⓒ 7 _____ = The crew traveled in small boats to Elephant Island.

Ⓓ 8 _____ days = Shackleton and five men sailed to the whaling station on South Georgia Island.

9 _____ hrs. = Shackleton and his men walked across South Georgia Island.

10 _____ = Shackleton rescued all of his men from Elephant Island.

D LISTEN FOR DETAILS Close your book. Watch the lecture again. Add details to your notes and correct any mistakes.

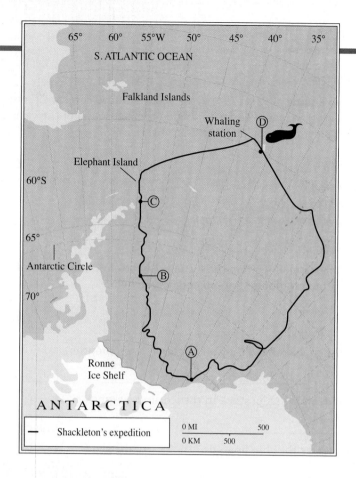

Map labels:
65° 60° 55°W 50° 45° 40° 35°

S. ATLANTIC OCEAN

Falkland Islands

Whaling station — D

Elephant Island

60°S

C

65°

Antarctic Circle

B

70°

A

Ronne Ice Shelf

ANTARCTICA

— Shackleton's expedition

0 MI 500
0 KM 500

E CHECK YOUR UNDERSTANDING Use your notes to decide if the statements are T (true) or F (false), based on the lecture. Correct the false statements.

_____ 1 Shackleton's goal was to sail around Antarctica.

_____ 2 The *Endurance*'s crew included ship's officers, sailors, and scientists.

_____ 3 Shackleton had crew members work together to get work done quickly.

_____ 4 In October 1915, the crew moved onto the ice because the ship was full.

_____ 5 When the crew reached Elephant Island, it was the first time in more than a year that they had stood on land.

_____ 6 Shackleton and five men traveled 80 miles by boat to South Georgia.

_____ 7 The South Georgia station manager thought Shackleton and his crew were dead.

_____ 8 Shackleton rescued his crew on Elephant Island right away.

HEAR the language

Linking: -ed Endings

In spoken English, the **-ed ending** of past tense verbs is pronounced three different ways: /d/, /t/, and /ɪd/. The pronunciation of -ed changes depending on the last sound of the verb. Learning to recognize -ed verb endings will help you hear past tense verbs.

EXAMPLES	
In January 1915, they **entered** the Antarctic Circle.	/d/
However, he never **reached** this goal.	/t/
But Shackleton **needed** everyone to work as a team.	/ɪd/

A LISTEN Listen to the statements from the lecture. Pay attention to the boldfaced past tense verbs. Check (✓) the pronunciation of the -ed ending you hear.

	/d/	/t/	/ɪd/
1 Shackleton and his crew **realized** they'd have to wait ten months until November.			
2 So, there they **lived**, on the ship, stuck in the ice, and waiting for spring.			
3 Over the long winter, as the ship **floated** with the ice, the ice began to crush the ship.			
4 He promised his men that if they **worked** hard and stayed together, they would get home.			
5 Because of the way he **treated** the men—treating each man with respect—the crew became extremely loyal.			
6 If Shackleton **believed** they would get home, well, the men **believed** it, too.			
7 He **decided** to take one of their small boats and sail back to a whaling station on South Georgia.			
8 And when they **walked** inside, as the story goes, the station manager took one look at these guys and said, "Who are you?"			
9 Over the next four months, Shackleton **tried** three times to rescue the men back on Elephant Island.			
10 For this, Shackleton is **credited** as one of the great heroes of the time.			

B PAIR WORK Practice saying the sentences with a partner. Be sure to pronounce the -ed endings correctly.

TALK about the topic

Keeping a Discussion on Topic

A FOLLOW THE DISCUSSION Watch as the students talk about Shackleton's journey. Read each opinion. Then check (✓) who agrees with it. More than one student may agree.

	Mia	Manny	Hannah	River
1 Shackleton was a great leader because he treated everyone equally.	☐	☐	☐	☐
2 Shackleton was a great leader because he made important decisions.	☐	☐	☐	☐

What are the students doing in their discussion of the lecture? Circle one or more.

a clarifying information   **b** sharing their opinions   **c** paraphrasing the ideas

B LEARN THE STRATEGIES Listen to the discussion again. Complete the comments with the phrases you hear. Then check (✓) the discussion strategy that the student uses.

there's no doubt that	I'd say	we're supposed to be	I'm curious about

	Asking for opinions or ideas	Expressing an opinion	Keeping a discussion on topic
1 River: "Guys, I think _____ talking about the lecture we heard today."	☐	☐	☐
2 Manny: "_____ that without great leadership, the ending would've been totally different."	☐	☐	☐
3 Hannah: "Yeah, so, _____ everyone's thoughts ... "	☐	☐	☐
4 Mia: "Hm, _____ his treatment of everyone as equals."	☐	☐	☐

Discussion Strategy In study groups or other organized conversations, **keeping the discussion on topic** is sometimes difficult. Tangents (related topics) can be interesting, but it's important to remind others to focus on the main topic of your discussion. You can remind others by using expressions such as *I'd like to get back to ...* , *We're getting a little off track ...* , and the very informal *Anyway*!

C TRY IT In a small group, discuss one or more of these quotations. What does it mean? Would Shackleton and his crew agree with it? Try to use the discussion strategies.

- "Exploration is the essence of the human spirit."—Frank Borman, astronaut
- "To lead people, walk beside them."—Lao-Tzu, Chinese philosopher
- "The first task of a leader is to keep hope alive."—Joe Batten, author
- "To be a leader, a person must have followers. And to have followers, a person must have their trust."—Dwight D. Eisenhower, US president

REVIEW your notes

REVIEW Work with a partner. Complete the timeline with dates and important events in the story of Shackleton and the *Endurance*. Use your notes from the lecture.

Endurance / Timeline

• 1914 _____

• _____

• 1915 _____

• _____

• _____

• _____

• 1916 _____

• _____

• _____

• _____

TIP!
A timeline can help you see the chronological order of events. It can also help you see "the big picture," or how individual events look all together.

 Now you are ready to take the Unit Test and the Proficiency Assessment

EXPRESS your ideas

An Important Event in My Life

In this unit, you learned about the story of Ernest Shackleton's journey to Antarctica. Obviously, Shackleton's journey to Antarctica was an "epic" event in his life. What "epic" or major events have you had in your life?

TASK **Give a short presentation about an interesting or important event in your life, using an object or picture that reminds you of the event. Work with a partner to prepare and practice.**

Prepare

1 Brainstorm. Think of an interesting or important event from your past.

2 Choose a visual aide to show the audience that reminds you of the event. It can be a souvenir (an object you kept to remember the event), a picture of an object, or a picture of a place.

3 Make a timeline of the events in the order they happened.

4 Ask your partner these questions:

- *When did the event happen? Where did it take place? Who were you with?*

- *What happened? Describe the events in chronological order.*

- *Why does the souvenir or picture remind you of the event?*

- *Why was this an important event in your life? What did you learn from the experience?*

5 Make an outline.

Practice

6 Practice with your partner. Practice using past tense, dates, time expressions, and sequencing expressions to make the order of events clear.

7 Practice by yourself.

Present

8 Deliver your presentation to the class. Use past tense, dates, time expressions, and sequencing expressions to make the order of events clear.

9 As you listen to your classmates' presentations:

- Take notes on the main ideas of each presentation. Note which stories are the happiest, most exciting, or most surprising.

- Write one question to ask each presenter.

Evaluate

10 After all the presentations are finished, discuss the information, including: *Which story is the happiest? The most exciting? The most surprising? Which presenter learned the most from the experience?*

11 Use the *Unit 10 Presentation Evaluation Form* (in Appendix C) to evaluate your classmates' presentations.

Presentation Strategy: Telling a story

Use dates or time expressions to show • when events happened. • how long events lasted.	*On January twentieth, twenty-sixteen …* *Two years ago …* *Last week …* *For two days / more than three hours / nearly a week*
Use sequencing expressions to show the order of events.	*First, … ,* *Next, … ,* *After that, … ,* *Suddenly, … ,* *Finally, …*
Use the past tense to show the story happened in the past.	*I took a trip with my family.*

OUTLINE: AN IMPORTANT EVENT IN MY LIFE

I Introduction: Introduce the souvenir or picture that reminds you of this event and describe it

II The important event

   Explain when the event happened, where it took place, and who you were with

   Tell the story of the event. Describe what happened in chronological order

III Conclusion: Explain why this was an important event in your life, and what you learned from it

IV Interaction: Answer questions from the audience

11 Ethics

CONNECT to the topic

Ethics are rules that help people decide what is right and wrong. We learn ethics from our family, religion, and culture. Philosophers study ethics and try to describe how people make ethical decisions.

A THINK ABOUT IT Read each situation. What would be the ethical thing to do? Compare answers with a partner.

- Rita finds an envelope on the ground. Inside the envelope is $1,000 in cash. There is a name and address on the envelope.

  a Return the money to the owner
  b Keep the money for herself

  c Other: _____

- A doctor tells Jim that he has a serious disease. Jim says he feels fine, but the doctor explains that the disease could spread easily to other people. The doctor tells Jim not to travel or spend time in crowded places. However, Jim already has bought tickets for a vacation to Europe, and he will lose his money if he cancels the trip.

  a Go on his vacation as planned
  b Cancel his vacation and stay home

  c Other: _____

B TUNE IN Listen to an interview with Muna Assiri, a professor of ethics. Then complete the sentences, based on the interview.

1 Ethics is a set of _____ that we can use to _____ what is right and wrong.

2 Professor Assiri uses an example of a child who needs _____.

3 Sometimes, a person's ethical rule _____ because the situation is not

_____.

C DISCUSS Discuss these questions in a small group: *Explain what you would do in the situations in Part A. Are your decisions ethical? Why or why not? How do you know whether an action is ethical or not?*

LEARNING OUTCOMES

In this unit you will:

- note real-world examples
- note the main ideas of a philosophy lecture
- note details from a philosophy lecture
- identify and practice pausing that separates ideas
- recognize and practice offering a fact or example
- review with a partner to prepare for the unit test
- give a presentation about an ethical problem, using pauses to make your ideas clear

BUILD your vocabulary

A LISTEN The boldfaced words are from the unit lecture on ethics. Listen to the sentences. Guess the meanings of the boldfaced words. Then match the words with their definitions.

_____ **1** It's important to think about how your **actions** affect other people. When you do something, consider the overall effect: Will it help or hurt them?

_____ **2** People can't smoke cigarettes in our office building, so the company **allows** employees to go outside to smoke.

_____ **3** My city **banned** cell phone use while driving. Drivers have to stop their cars to make cell phone calls.

    a stopped or disallowed
    b let someone do something
    c things you do

_____ **4** Government leaders should make decisions that are good for the whole **community**, not just some of the people.

_____ **5** We need to make our own **individual** decisions, not copy what everyone else does. For example, some people refuse to pay taxes.

_____ **6** A few people are against the new no-smoking law, but the **majority** support it.

    d as a single person, separate from the society one lives in
    e most of the people in a group
    f a group of people who live in the same area

_____ **7** It's important to have **freedom** to choose your religion. It's unethical for someone to tell you which religion to choose.

_____ **8** Governments should spend money where it will do the **greatest good** and help the most people.

_____ **9** I believe it is wrong to hurt or kill animals. Because of this **principle**, I don't eat meat.

    g the ability to do what you want, without being controlled by others
    h the most positive effect
    i a belief about what is right or wrong that affects how you behave

____ **10** The government gives the people the **right** of free speech. That means that people are free to say what they want, and the government can't stop them.

____ **11** We have to pay a **tax** on everything we buy. The government uses that extra money to pay for schools and roads.

____ **12** I wanted to buy cigarettes, but I made the more **utilitarian** choice and spent my last $20 on groceries.

    j money you must pay to the government for use in public services

    k something that you can ethically or legally do

    l useful

B PAIR WORK Work with a partner. Reorder the words and write the complete sentence. Take turns saying the sentences.

1 I believe in (**freedom** / make / **to** / choices / the).

_____

2 Every day individuals (**about** / **choices** / make / must) what is best.

_____

3 We don't always know (the **effects** / our actions / **of** / on) other people.

_____

4 Ethical principles (help / **decisions** / **make** / us / good).

_____

5 Sometimes utilitarian decisions serve (**in** / only / the greater good / **principle**).

_____

6 Some people want (to / free / **on** / put / speech / **ban** / a).

_____

7 However, most people believe in (the / free / **right** / **to** / speech).

_____

8 The (people / **of** / community / **majority** / in / my) agree with me.

_____

9 Many people (**issue** / have / **with** / an) smoking in public places.

_____

10 Every individual (**to** / **be** / should / **allowed** / enjoy) freedom of expression.

_____

FOCUS your attention

Real-World Examples

Speakers may use real-world examples to explain a general principle. A real-world example is a short story or situation based on something that we experience in everyday life.

PHRASES THAT SIGNAL A REAL-WORLD EXAMPLE

Let's look at a real-world example ...

Let's take as an example ...

Let's say that ...

QUESTIONS THAT SIGNAL A REAL-WORLD EXAMPLE

Speakers may also ask questions with *What* or *How* about the real-world example:

What would you do?

What about ... ?

How does this affect ... ?

How do we make a decision ... ?

A TRY IT Listen to an excerpt from a lecture on ethics. Listen for the real-world example and the questions. Complete the notes below.

Ethical _____ — right / wrong

 e.g. _____

   Clerk — _____ — too much $

   Do you _____ $

   OR _____ $ back?

 Ethics — everyday lives

B PAIR WORK Compare notes with a partner.

WATCH the lecture

A **THINK ABOUT IT** You're about to watch the unit lecture on ethical decision making. The speaker discusses two approaches: the rights approach and the utilitarian approach. Based on the meanings of the words *rights* and *utilitarian*, how do you think these two terms will be defined?

The rights approach: An ethical decision is an action that is

_____ .

The utilitarian approach: An ethical decision is an action that is

_____ .

Professor Robert Myers

B **LISTEN FOR MAIN IDEAS** Close your book. Watch the lecture and take notes.

C **CHECK YOUR UNDERSTANDING** Use your notes. Circle the best answer, based on the lecture.

1 According to the rights approach, an ethical decision must _____ .
  a be agreed to by each individual
  b help the most people
  c respect an individual's choices

2 According to the utilitarian approach, an ethical decision must _____ .
  a be good for each individual
  b create the greatest good for the community
  c give people the right to make choices

3 The professor gives the example of smoking in public to illustrate _____ .
  a the rights approach
  b the utilitarian approach
  c the difference between the rights and utilitarian approaches

4 The professor suggests that _____ to make a decision about public smoking.
  a the rights approach works best
  b the utilitarian approach works best
  c the rights and utilitarian approaches work equally well

D **LISTEN FOR DETAILS** Close your book. Watch the lecture again. Add details to your notes and correct any mistakes.

E CHECK YOUR UNDERSTANDING Use your notes. Check (√) the approach that the sentence is describing, based on the lecture.

	Individual rights	Utilitarianism
1 This idea is from the philosophy of Immanuel Kant.	√	
2 This idea was made popular by John Stuart Mill.		√
3 People must respect an individual's freedom to speak.		
4 Individuals must pay taxes to help the community.		
5 What action will mean the greatest good?		
6 How does this affect a person's freedom to choose?		
7 Smokers should be free to smoke because everyone is free to make his or her own decisions about health.		
8 Nonsmokers should be free to breathe clean air because smoking is bad for public health.		
9 Smoking should be allowed in order to please smokers.		
10 Smoking creates a lot of health problems for the community, so it should be banned.		
11 Smoking should be banned if we want to save money in our health care system.		

HEAR the language

Pausing That Separates Ideas

As we saw in Unit 5, speakers separate their ideas into "thought groups." When you hear a pause, you can try to identify a key idea, and then listen for the next idea.

Speakers may pause before or after

- signal words or phrases (*then, however, in fact, because*).
- items in a list.
- an important word or new term.

Learning to hear "thought groups" will help you follow the speaker's ideas.

> **EXAMPLE**
> *Today / I'd like to talk about two different approaches / two different ways to make ethical decisions / the rights approach / and the utilitarian approach /*

A LISTEN Listen to the statements and questions from the lecture. Notice when the speaker pauses between thought groups. Write a slash (/) where you hear a pause. Note that punctuation indicating a pause has been removed.

1 This idea of rights comes originally from the philosophy of Immanuel Kant a German philosopher in the 18th century

2 Freedom of speech means two things first that I have the right to say whatever I want and second that other people must respect my right to speak

3 To decide if an action is ethical using the rights approach we must always ask How does this action affect the individual's freedom to make choices

4 The utilitarian approach was made popular in the 19th century by British philosopher John Stuart Mill

5 In this approach the most important thing is not individual rights

6 Now most people don't like paying taxes because they have less money to spend on other things

7 Now let's take a real-world example and look at how to make a decision using these two approaches that is the rights approach and the utilitarian approach

8 When you look at the problem from the rights approach we have to ask How does smoking in public affect individual rights

9 This however shows us one of the problems of using the rights approach because when you have two groups how do you decide whose rights are more important smokers' or nonsmokers'

10 Following that approach we have to ask What creates the greatest amount of good

B PAIR WORK Practice saying the sentences with a partner. Be sure to pause between groups of words.

TALK about the topic

Offering a Fact or Example

🔊 ⏹ **A FOLLOW THE DISCUSSION** Watch as the students talk about ethics. Read each opinion. Then check (√) who agrees with it. More than one student may agree.

Michael   May   Yhinny   Qiang

	Michael	May	Yhinny	Qiang
1 People should have the right to talk on a cell phone while driving.	☐	☐	☐	☐
2 Drivers using cell phones are dangerous.	☐	☐	☐	☐

What are the students doing in their discussion of the lecture? Circle one or more.

a clarifying the ideas   **b** giving relevant examples   **c** defining terms

🔊 ⏹ **B LEARN THE STRATEGIES** Watch the discussion again. Complete the comments with words and phrases you hear. Then check (√) the discussion strategy that the student uses.

I mean	personally	well	something like

	Expressing an opinion	Offering a fact or example
1 Qiang: "Well, _____, I believe I should have the right to talk on the phone while I'm in my car."	☐	☐
2 Qiang: "_____, talking on the phone doesn't really hurt anyone's health."	☐	☐
3 Michael: "Drivers using cell phones have _____ four times more accidents."	☐	☐
4 May: "OK, _____, lots of drivers pay more attention to their phone conversations than the road, which is dangerous, right?"	☐	☐

Discussion Strategy By **offering a fact or example**, you can support your opinion and add new information on a topic. This can make the topic more understandable and more memorable. Personal experiences (*In my experience ...*), observations (*I've noticed ...*), and media (*I just read this article in the Times ...*) are a few ways you can begin.

C TRY IT In a small group, discuss one or more of these topics. Try to use the discussion strategies.

- Think about the ethical decisions from the unit. Do you agree or disagree with the positions discussed in the lecture and student discussion? Why or why not?

- Think of your own example of an ethical decision. Analyze it using the rights approach and the utilitarian approach. Which approach leads to the best decision? Why?

REVIEW your notes

REVIEW Work with a partner. Add details to these notes about the two ethical approaches discussed in the lecture. Use your notes from the lecture.

	Rights approach	Utilitarian approach
1st per. to describe this approach:		
Ex. of this approach:		
Most important thing about this approach:		
How this approach sees / addresses public smoking:		

> **TIP!**
> Try adding your own examples. This can make your notes more interesting and help you better understand a new concept.

 Now you are ready to take the Unit Test and the Proficiency Assessment.

EXPRESS your ideas

An Ethical Decision

In this unit, you have learned about two approaches to ethical decision making—the "rights" approach and the "utilitarian" approach. Do these approaches help you make decisions in complicated situations?

TASK **Give a short presentation about an ethical problem and possible decisions about the problem. Apply one of the ethical approaches to a new example. Work with a partner to prepare and practice.**

Prepare

1 Brainstorm. Think of an ethical problem that affects you personally or society in general. Ask your partner some of these questions:

- *What is the ethical problem?*
- *Which people or groups does the problem affect? How does it affect them?*
- *Analyzing the problem using the rights approach and the utilitarian approach: How does it affect an individual's rights? How does it affect the greater good?*
- *What is the most ethical decision?*

2 Write your ideas in a chart, showing the ethical problem, two possible decisions, and how the two possible decisions affect people. Then decide on the best ethical decision.

3 Make an outline.

Practice

4 Practice with your partner. Practice pausing between ideas.

5 Practice by yourself.

Present

6 Deliver your presentation to the class. Pause between ideas.

7 As you listen to your classmates' presentations:

- Take notes on the main ideas of each presentation. Note which ethical decisions you agree or disagree with.
- Write one question to ask each presenter.

Evaluate

8 After all the presentations are finished, discuss the information, including: *Which ethical problem is the most difficult to make a decision about? Do you agree or disagree with the presenters' choice of the most ethical decision? Why?*

9 Use the *Unit 11 Presentation Evaluation Form* (in Appendix C) to evaluate your classmates' presentations.

Presentation Strategy: Pausing between ideas

When you present, it is important not to speak too quickly (see Unit 4). One way to slow your speech is to pause between ideas or thought groups. Pausing signals that you are introducing a new idea. It also gives the listener time to understand what you have just said.

- Pause after signal words.
- Pause before contrasting ideas (signaled by words such as *but, however, although*) and before conjunctions (*and, so*).
- Pause at the ends of sentences.

OUTLINE: AN ETHICAL DECISION

I Introduction: Explain the ethical problem

II The ethical decision

Explain the first decision and how it affects people

Explain the second decision and how it affects people

III Conclusion: Recommend the best ethical decision and explain why this is the best decision

IV Interaction: Answer questions from the audience

12 Big Data

CONNECT to the topic

Information technology is the study or use of computers and other equipment to collect, store, organize, communicate, and use information, or data. Data scientists study data to help businesses and organizations solve problems.

A THINK ABOUT IT Individuals create about 75 percent of all digital data. This data is collected every time we use social media, do an Internet search, or buy something online. Look at the list of personal information. What information do you think is OK to be collected and stored by businesses or the government? What information should not be? Why? Discuss your responses with a partner.

- Your address and telephone number
- Where you are right now
- Where you go to school or work
- The names of your family members and friends

- The amount of money you have
- Things you buy online or in the store
- The videos you watch
- Your medical history

B TUNE IN Listen to an interview with data scientist Sonia Chen. Match the unit of digital data with the amount of information it measures. Not all of the units of information will be used.

_____ 1 one letter of the alphabet, such as a, b, or c

_____ 2 one medium-sized book

_____ 3 about 1,000 books

_____ 4 all of the books in a large library

a byte

b kilobyte (KB)

c megabyte (MB)

d gigabyte (GB)

e terabyte (TB)

f petabyte (PB)

g exabyte (EB)

h zettabyte (ZB)

i yottabyte (YB)

C DISCUSS Discuss these questions in a small group: _How much data do you think you have stored on your computer(s) or electronic devices? Can others collect that data? How?_

LEARNING OUTCOMES
In this unit you will:
- note the general point of a personal story
- note main ideas from an information technology lecture
- fact-check statements about an information technology lecture
- identify and practice repeated words and word patterns
- recognize and practice strategies for keeping a discussion going
- discuss the lecture with a partner to prepare for the unit test
- give a presentation about the pros and cons of a type of technology, and include an introduction and conclusion

BUILD your vocabulary

A LISTEN The boldfaced words are from the unit lecture on big data. Listen to each passage. Read along. Guess the meanings of the boldfaced words. Then match the words with their definitions.

Data mining is the process of looking at data and summarizing it into useful information. This information can be used to make decisions and solve problems, such as helping a business save money or increase sales. The data is first **captured** and stored. For example, a shop might save records of its customers' purchases. Then data scientists use special software programs to **analyze** the data. They look at **sequences** of data to try to find **patterns**. For instance, a business can look at its customers' purchases over time to find out their buying habits.

ANALYSIS

___ 1 captured	**a** things that happens in a regular and repeated way
___ 2 analyze	**b** groups of things that come right after another
___ 3 sequences	**c** got and put information into a form that can be read or used by a computer
___ 4 patterns	**d** look at something carefully to understand it

After studying data, data scientists create a **model** that describes it. Since groups of data are large and **complex**, data needs to be put into a format that is easy to understand. This involves **converting** the information into an infographic—a chart or image of the information patterns. The data can be used to predict and make plans for the future. For example, a store could use data to make a **forecast** of future sales.

___ 5 model	**e** a prediction of the future
___ 6 complex	**f** changing something into a different form
___ 7 converting	**g** a description of something
___ 8 forecast	**h** not easy to understand or

$\longrightarrow$

Once a business has **access** to our data, it can be used to make decisions. For example, a shopping website can follow the **trail** of a customer's online purchases. If a customer buys a new suitcase and a language course, that person may be planning a trip. The company can send the customer advertisements for other travel products or share the information with other companies. This raises new concerns about our **privacy**—how much information do companies collect about us? What happens to this information? Is this information **accurate**, or does it contain mistakes?

_____ 9 **access**	**i** signs that are left behind by someone that can be followed
_____ 10 **trail**	**j** freedom from public attention
_____ 11 **privacy**	**k** correct or exact
_____ 12 **accurate**	**l** ability to get or use something

B PAIR WORK Work in pairs. Student A: Read aloud sentence starters 1–6 from Column 1. Student B: Listen and complete each sentence with a phrase from Column 2. Notice the boldfaced words. Switch roles for 7–12.

COLUMN 1	COLUMN 2
1 Data about customers' shopping habits is **collected**	**a by** technology.
2 Data analysts **look**	**b into** digital data.
3 They **convert information**	**c for** patterns.
4 The alphabet is a **sequence**	**d for** future use.
5 Businesses **store data**	**e of** letters.
6 We are all **affected**	**f by** online businesses.
7 I **applied**	**g on** my phone.
8 I checked the **app**	**h for** a new job.
9 I took a new **route**	**i to** privacy.
10 The thief left a **trail**	**j to pay** for committing the crime.
11 I don't want to lose my **right**	**k of** evidence.
12 There will be a **price**	**l to** school today.

FOCUS your attention

Personal Stories

Speakers often use personal stories to explain a point. Although the story may be about an event that happened to just him or her, the speaker's purpose is to make a general point.

As a listener, you must listen for the general point the speaker is making. If the speaker does not state the point directly, you have to make an *inference* about it. An inference is a guess based on the available information. Be sure to write the general points in your notes.

TELLING AND SUMMARIZING PERSONAL STORIES

- When telling a personal story, the speaker may use *I* and past tense verbs.
- When summarizing the general point of the story, the speaker may use *we* or *us* and present tense verbs.

A TRY IT Listen to an introduction from a lecture on big data. What personal story does the speaker tell? What is the general point the speaker is trying to make?

Data use

Streaming _____ – 30 mins, _____ MB

Email – 25 _____ , 7 MB

_____ – 30 mins, 8K MB

each activity = _____

B PAIR WORK Compare notes with a partner.

WATCH the lecture

A THINK ABOUT IT You're about to watch the unit lecture on big data. What do you think "big data" means? What types of businesses and organizations collect data? What are some uses of big data?

Big data is _____ .

It is collected by _____ .

It is used to _____ .

Professor Colin Edwards

B LISTEN FOR MAIN IDEAS Close your book. Watch the lecture and take notes.

C CHECK YOUR UNDERSTANDING Use your notes to check (✓) the uses of big data mentioned in the lecture. Two uses are not mentioned.

☐ **1** Finding interesting news stories

☐ **2** Finding out what friends are reading

☐ **3** Making weather forecasts

☐ **4** Shopping for clothes online

☐ **5** Finding airplane flights and hotels

☐ **6** Predicting public health problems

☐ **7** Planning travel routes

D LISTEN FOR DETAILS Close your book. Watch the lecture again. Add details to your notes and correct any mistakes.

E **CHECK YOUR UNDERSTANDING** Use your notes. Mark the statements *T* (true) or *F* (false), based on the lecture. Correct the false statements.

_____ **1** "Big data" means groups of data that are very large or complex.

_____ **2** Insurance companies collect information about their patients' health habits.

_____ **3** Internet providers collect information about the websites you visit.

_____ **4** Information becomes data when we analyze it.

_____ **5** Byte streams are patterns found in big groups of data.

_____ **6** Comparing data helps reduce the amount of data that is collected.

_____ **7** Analyzing weather patterns helps weather scientists accurately predict the weather.

_____ **8** News websites analyze reading patterns of people to find out their interests.

_____ **9** The speaker told a story about using his app to plan a trip.

_____ **10** We leave a trail of evidence every time we use our phones.

HEAR the language

Sentence Rhythm: Repetition

Speakers in English may **repeat** words or patterns of words. In lectures or public speaking, speakers use repetition to create a dramatic effect so that listeners pay more attention. Repetition can also emphasize a point or idea. When speakers repeat phrases, the stress falls on the repeated word or the new information in the word pattern.

EXAMPLES	
Repeated words	**Repeated word patterns**
over and _over_	It depends on _where_ to buy it, _how much_ it costs, _what_ it's made of. (wh- clauses)

A LISTEN Listen to the statements and questions from the lecture. Fill in the repeated words or word patterns. Listen for the rhythm of stressed words in the repetition.

1 Well, _____ collect information about their customers' credit card purchases. _____ _____ collect information about their patients' visits to

   the doctor. _____ _____ collect information about what websites you visit.

2 And the list goes _____ and _____ .

3 _____ you _____ , _____ you _____ , _____ you like, even _____ you like—it's all collected by someone.

4 Information becomes data when _____ _____ it, when _____ _____ it for future use.

5 Once the data is stored in byte streams, we can then use special software programs to _____ and _____ it—to _____ patterns, and _____ models.

6 This creates _____ _____ . _____ and _____ _____ every moment.

7 Forecasts come from weather scientists who collect large amounts of _____ data—like _____ changes and _____ movement.

8 Every time we _____ our _____ , _____ a _____ _____ _____ , or _____ the _____ , we leave a trail of evidence.

9 Same thing when you apply for a _____ _____ , or _____ , or a _____ .

10 But is this fair? _____ can _____ this data? _____ can _____ this data? And is the information about you accurate?

B PAIR WORK Practice saying the sentences with a partner. Be sure to repeat the patterns with the correct rhythm of stressed and unstressed words.

TALK about the topic

Keeping a Discussion Going

A FOLLOW THE DISCUSSION Watch as the students talk about the lecture on big data. Read each opinion. Then check (✓) who agrees with it. More than one student may agree.

Shelley   Hugh   Kenzie   Ben

	Shelley	Hugh	Kenzie	Ben
1 I'm surprised that we use big data so often.	☐	☐	☐	☐
2 The lecture included a lot of examples.	☐	☐	☐	☐
3 I'm impressed at how fast big data is growing.	☐	☐	☐	☐

What are the students doing in their discussion of the lecture? Circle one or more.

a sharing opinions   **b** discussing relevant examples   **c** defining terms

B LEARN THE STRATEGIES Watch the discussion again. Complete the comments with the words and phrases you hear. Then check (✓) the discussion strategy that the student uses. More than one answer may be possible.

me, too	right	surprised by	what about you

	Agreeing	Keeping a discussion going
1 Shelley: "Were you guys _____ anything?"	☐	☐
2 Hugh: "Yeah. _____ . That was interesting."	☐	☐
3 Shelley: "Hugh, _____ ? What impressed you?"	☐	☐
4 Ben: "_____ , I mean the amount of data, just growing all the time ... "	☐	☐

Discussion Strategy: It's important to help **keep a discussion going** by encouraging people to talk. One approach is to ask follow-up questions to get more information or clarification about an idea. Another approach is to ask a specific person to answer a question. This encourages less-talkative people to join in the discussion.

C TRY IT In a small group, discuss one or more of these topics. Try to use the discussion strategies.

- Can you think of any other examples of everyday situations where we get information from big data?

- How do you feel about the use of big data? Do you appreciate the information we get from big data? Are you worried about privacy issues?

- How comfortable are you with your data being used in all the examples in the lecture?

REVIEW your notes

REVIEW Read your notes. Did you write down key words and their meanings? Can you explain the main ideas of the lecture? Work with a partner to discuss and complete these notes.

Big Data	
Data	= Info, _____
Big data	= Large, _____ data
	1. _____
	2. _____
	3. _____
1. _____	_____
Who?	What you _____
	Information → Data when _____
	Digitization _____
Data increasing	Software _____
	2 x _____
2. _____	Benefits – individual
Weather report	_____
_____	_____
_____	_____
	_____
	_____
	_____
	_____
3. _____	- right to privacy _____
B.D. follows us	- leave a trail
	- data miners _____

TIPS!
- Use the space on the page to organize your notes.
- Write main ideas down the left side of the page. Indent (add a few spaces) before subtopics under the main ideas.
- Write the details on the right side.
- Start a new line for a new idea.

 Now you are ready to take the Unit Test and the Proficiency Assessment.

EXPRESS your ideas

Benefits and Risks of Technology

In this unit, you have learned about the collection and use of big data. Do you think that the collection of big data has more benefits than risks?

TASK Give a short presentation about the benefits and risks of one type of technology. Work with a partner to prepare and practice.

Prepare

1 Choose a type of technology that you use or benefit from in your life.

airplanes	robots
cars	smart phones
computers / laptops	tablets
game players	your idea: _____
music players	

2 Think about how the technology affects you. Think of personal stories to explain your points.

- *What are the benefits of the technology? How can it make your life better?*
- *What are some potential problems or risks with the technology?*

3 Make an outline.

Practice

4 Practice with your partner. Practice your introduction and conclusion.

5 Practice by yourself.

Present

6 Deliver your presentation to the class. Include an introduction and conclusion.

7 As you listen to your classmates' presentations note the technology that you think has the most benefits and the most problems.

Evaluate

8 After all the presentations are finished, discuss the information, including: *Which type of technology has the most benefits? Which type has the most problems or risks?*

9 Use the *Unit 12 Presentation Evaluation Form* (in Appendix C) to evaluate your classmates' presentations.

Presentation Strategy: Introducing and concluding your presentation

To introduce your presentation:

A) Greet your audience:
> *Good morning …*
> *Hello everyone …*

B) Choose a way to get your audience's attention:
- Ask a question:
> *How many of you … ?*
> *What do you think about … ?*

OR • Tell an interesting fact or story:
> *Did you know that … ?*
> *The other day …*

OR • Show an interesting picture about the topic:
> *Look at this …*

C) Introduce your topic:
> *Today I'd like to talk about …*

To conclude your presentation:

D) Make a statement about your most important point or what you want the audience to remember:
> *So, just remember …*
> *Next time you … think about …*
> *I'd like to end by saying …*
> *To wrap up, I'd like to say …*

E) Invite the audience to ask you questions:
> *Do you have any questions?*
> *Can I answer any questions?*

OUTLINE: BENEFITS AND RISKS OF A TECHNOLOGY

I Introduction:
  Greet your audience and get their attention
  Introduce the technology and explain how it is used

II Benefits and risks of the technology
  Describe one way you benefit from the technology
  Describe a second way you benefit from it
  Describe the potential problems or risks

III Conclusion: Advise about how we should use the technology

IV Interaction: Answer audience questions

Academic Word List

Numbers indicate the sublist of the Academic Word List. For example, *abandon* and its family members are in Sublist 8. Sublist 1 contains the most frequent words in the list, and Sublist 10 contains the least frequent. **Boldfacing** indicates that the word is taught in *Contemporary Topics* 1. The page number of the section where the word is taught is indicated in parentheses.

abandon	8	anticipate	9	bulk	9	compile	10
abstract	6	apparent	4	capable	6	complement	8
academy	5	append	8	capacity	5	**complex** (p. 113)	2
access (p. 113)	4	appreciate	8	**category** (p. 43)	2	component	3
accommodate	9	**approach** (p. 33)	1	cease	9	compound	5
accompany	8	appropriate	2	challenge	5	comprehensive	7
accumulate	8	approximate	4	channel	7	comprise	7
accurate (p. 113)	6	arbitrary	8	chapter	2	compute	2
achieve (p. 3)	2	area	1	chart	8	conceive	10
acknowledge	6	**aspect** (p. 23)	2	chemical	7	**concentrate** (p. 33)	4
acquire (p. 13)	2	assemble	10	**circumstance** (p. 33)	3	concept	1
adapt	7	assess	1	cite	6	conclude	2
adequate	4	assign	6	civil	4	concurrent	9
adjacent	10	assist	2	clarify	8	conduct	2
adjust	5	assume	1	classic	7	**confer** (p. 33)	4
administrate	2	assure	9	clause	5	confine	9
adult	7	attach	6	code	4	confirm	7
advocate	7	attain	9	coherent	9	**conflict** (p. 33)	5
affect	2	attitude	4	coincide	9	conform	8
aggregate	6	attribute	4	collapse	10	consent	3
aid	7	author	6	colleague	10	**consequent** (p. 23)	2
albeit	10	authority	1	commence	9	considerable	3
allocate	6	**automate** (p. 53)	8	comment	3	consist	1
alter	5	available	1	commission	2	constant	3
alternative	3	aware	5	commit	4	constitute	1
ambiguous	8	behalf	9	commodity	8	constrain	3
amend	5	**benefit** (p. 33)	1	**communicate** (p. 43)	4	construct	2
analogy	9	bias	8	**community** (p. 103)	2	consult	5
analyze (p. 113)	1	bond	6	compatible	9	**consume** (p. 73)	2
annual	4	brief	6	compensate	3	contact	5

contemporary	8	despite	4	ensure	3	fluctuate	8
context	1	detect	8	entity	5	**focus** (p. 83)	2
contract	1	deviate	8	**environment** (p. 13)	1	format	9
contradict	8	device	9	equate	2	formula	1
contrary	7	devote	9	equip	7	forthcoming	10
contrast	4	differentiate	7	equivalent	5	found	9
contribute	3	dimension	4	erode	9	foundation	7
controversy	9	diminish	9	error	4	framework	3
convene	3	discrete	5	establish	1	**function** (p. 23)	1
converse	9	discriminate	6	estate	6	fund	3
convert (p. 113)	7	displace	8	estimate	1	fundamental	5
convince	10	display	6	**ethic** (p. 103)	9	furthermore	6
cooperate	6	dispose	7	ethnic	4	gender	6
coordinate	3	distinct	2	evaluate	2	generate	5
core	3	distort	9	eventual	8	generation	5
corporate	3	distribute	1	evident	1	globe	7
correspond	3	**diverse** (p. 83)	6	evolve	5	**goal** (p. 3)	4
couple	7	document	3	exceed	6	grade	7
create (p. 43)	1	domain	6	exclude	3	grant	4
credit (p. 93)	2	domestic	4	exhibit	8	guarantee	7
criteria	3	dominate	3	expand	5	guideline	8
crucial	8	draft	5	expert	6	hence	4
culture	2	drama	8	explicit	6	hierarchy	7
currency	8	duration	9	exploit	8	highlight	8
cycle	4	dynamic	7	export	1	hypothesis	4
data (p. 3)	1	economy	1	expose	5	identical	7
debate	4	edit	6	external	5	**identify** (p. 83)	1
decade	7	element	2	extract	7	ideology	7
decline	5	eliminate	7	facilitate	5	ignorance	6
deduce	3	**emerge** (p. 43)	4	**factor** (p. 13)	1	illustrate	3
define	1	emphasis	3	feature	2	**image** (p. 43)	5
definite	7	empirical	7	federal	6	immigrate	3
demonstrate	3	enable	5	fee	6	**impact** (p. 23)	2
denote	8	encounter	10	file	7	**implement** (p. 83)	4
deny	7	energy	5	**final** (p. 93)	2	implicate	4
depress (p. 63)	10	enforce	5	finance	1	implicit	8
derive	1	enhance	6	finite	7	imply	3
design (p. 82)	2	enormous	10	flexible	6	impose	4

incentive	6	investigate	4	minimal	9	parallel	4
incidence	6	invoke	10	minimize	8	parameter	4
incline	10	**involve** (p. 63)	1	minimum	6	**participate** (p. 83)	2
income (p. 3)	1	isolate	7	ministry	6	partner	3
incorporate	6	issue	1	minor	3	passive	9
index	6	item	2	mode	7	perceive	2
indicate	1	**job** (p. 93)	4	**modify** (p. 73)	5	**percent** (p. 23)	1
individual (p. 103)	1	journal	2	monitor	5	**period** (p. 13)	1
induce	8	justify	3	**motive** (p. 13)	6	persist	10
inevitable	8	label	4	mutual	9	perspective	5
infer	7	labor	1	negate	3	**phase** (p. 83)	4
infrastructure	8	layer	3	network	5	phenomenon	7
inherent	9	lecture	6	neutral	6	**philosophy** (p. 102)	3
inhibit	6	legal	1	nevertheless	6	physical	3
initial	3	legislate	1	nonetheless	10	plus	8
initiate	6	levy	10	norm	9	policy	1
injure (p. 23)	2	liberal	5	**normal** (p. 73)	2	portion	9
innovate (p. 83)	7	license	5	notion	5	pose	10
input	6	likewise	10	notwithstanding	10	**positive** (p. 2)	2
insert	7	**link** (p. 23)	3	nuclear	8	**potential** (p. 63)	2
insight	9	**locate**	3	objective	5	practitioner	8
inspect	8	logic	5	**obtain** (p. 53)	2	precede	6
instance	3	maintain	2	**obvious** (p. 13)	4	precise	5
institute	2	**major** (p. 103)	1	occupy	4	predict	4
instruct	6	manipulate	8	occur	1	predominant	8
integral	9	manual	9	odd	10	preliminary	9
integrate	4	margin	5	offset	8	presume	6
integrity	10	mature	9	ongoing	10	previous	2
intelligence	6	maximize	3	option	4	**primary** (p. 73)	2
intense	8	mechanism	4	orient	5	prime	5
interact (p. 62)	3	media	7	outcome	3	principal	4
intermediate	9	mediate	9	output	4	**principle** (p. 103)	1
internal	4	medical	5	**overall** (p. 103)	4	prior	4
interpret	1	medium	9	overlap	9	priority	7
interval	6	mental	5	overseas	6	proceed	1
intervene	7	**method** (p. 3)	1	panel	10	process	1
intrinsic	10	migrate	6	paradigm	7	professional	4
invest	2	military	9	paragraph	8	prohibit	7

project	4	respond	1	stable	5	thesis	7
promote	4	restore	8	statistic	4	topic	7
proportion	3	restrain	9	status	4	trace	6
prospect	8	restrict	2	straightforward	10	tradition (p. 43)	2
protocol	9	retain (p. 73)	4	strategy	2	transfer	2
psychology (p. 2)	5	reveal	6	stress	4	transform	6
publication	7	revenue	5	structure	1	transit	5
publish	3	reverse	7	style (p. 43)	5	transmit	7
purchase (p. 73)	2	revise (p. 83)	8	submit	7	transport	6
pursue	5	revolution	9	subordinate	9	trend	5
qualitative	9	rigid	9	subsequent	4	trigger	9
quote	7	role (p. 13)	1	subsidy	6	ultimate	7
radical	8	route	9	substitute	5	undergo	10
random	8	scenario	9	successor	7	underlie	6
range	2	schedule	8	sufficient	3	undertake	4
ratio	5	scheme	3	sum	4	uniform	8
rational	6	scope	6	summary	4	unify	9
react	3	section	1	supplement	9	unique	7
recover	6	sector	1	survey	2	utilize (p. 53)	6
refine	9	secure	2	survive (p. 93)	7	valid	3
regime	4	seek	2	suspend	9	vary	1
region	2	select	2	sustain	5	vehicle	8
register	3	sequence (p. 113)	3	symbol	5	version	5
regulate	2	series	4	tape	6	via	8
reinforce	8	sex	3	target	5	violate	9
reject	5	shift (p. 23)	3	task (p. 53)	3	virtual	8
relax	9	significant	1	team (p. 93)	9	visible	7
release	7	similar	1	technical	3	vision	9
relevant (p. 3)	2	simulate	7	technique (p. 43)	3	visual	8
reluctance	10	site	2	technology (p. 113)	3	volume	3
rely	3	so - called	10	temporary	9	voluntary	7
remove	3	sole	7	tense	8	welfare	5
require (p. 3)	1	somewhat	7	terminate	8	whereas	5
research (p. 3)	1	source (p. 73)	1	text	2	whereby	10
reside	2	specific	1	theme	8	widespread	8
resolve (p. 33)	4	specify	3	theory (p. 13)	1		
resource	2	sphere	9	thereby	8		

APPENDIX B

Affix Charts

Learning the meanings of affixes can help you identify unfamiliar words you read or hear. A *prefix* is a letter or group of letters at the beginning of a word. It usually changes the meaning. A *suffix* is a letter or group of letters at the end of a word. It usually changes the part of speech. The charts below contain common prefixes and suffixes. Refer to the charts as you use this book.

PREFIX	MEANING	EXAMPLE
a-, ab-, il-, im-, in-, ir-, un-	not, without	atypical, abnormal illegal, impossible, inconvenient, irregular, unfair
anti-	opposed to, against	antisocial, antiseptic
co-, col-, com-, con-, cor-	with, together	coexist, collect, commune, connect, correct
de-	give something the opposite quality	decriminalize
dis-	not, remove	disapprove, disarm
ex-	no longer, former	ex-wife, ex-president
ex-	out, from	export, exit
extra-	outside, beyond	extracurricular, extraordinary
in-, im-	in, into	incoming, import
inter-	between, among	international
post-	later than, after	postgraduate
pro-	in favor of	pro-education
semi-	half, partly	semicircle, semi-literate
sub-	under, below, less important	subway, submarine, subordinate
super-	larger, greater, stronger	supermarket, supervisor

SUFFIX	MEANING	EXAMPLE
-able, -ible	having the quality of, capable of (adj)	comfortable, responsible
-al, -ial	relating to (adj)	professional, ceremonial
-ence, -ance, -ency, -ancy,	the act, state, or quality of (n)	intelligence, performance, competency, conservancy
-ation, -tion, -ion	the act, state, or result of (n)	examination, selection, facilitation
-er, -or, -ar, -ist	someone who does a particular thing (n)	photographer, editor, beggar, psychologist
-ful	full of (adj)	beautiful, harmful, fearful
-ify, -ize	give something a particular quality (v)	clarify, modernize
-ility	the quality of (n)	affordability, responsibility, humility
-ism	a political or religious belief system (n)	atheism, capitalism
-ist	relating to (or someone who has) a political or religious belief (adj, n)	Buddhist, socialist
-ive, -ous, -ious,	having a particular quality (adj)	creative, dangerous, mysterious
-ity	a particular quality (n)	popularity, creativity
-less	without (adj)	careless, worthless
-ly	in a particular way (adj, adv)	briefly, fluently
-ment	conditions that result from something (n)	government, development
-ness	quality of (n)	happiness, seriousness

APPENDIX C

Student Presentation Evaluation Forms for Express Your Ideas

UNIT 1

EVALUATION FORM: Showing confidence

Use this form to evaluate your classmates' presentations. Then share your feedback in groups.

1 - Strongly Disagree, 2 - Disagree, 3 - Agree, 4 - Strongly Agree	1	2	3	4
The presenter looked at the audience while speaking.				
The presenter showed confidence in body language.				
The presenter spoke loud enough.				
The presenter spoke clearly.				
The presenter explained ideas clearly.				

Total: _____

Suggest 3 ways the presenter might improve his or her future presentations.

1 _____

2 _____

3 _____

UNIT 2

EVALUATION FORM: Involving your audience with questions

Use this form to evaluate your classmates' presentations. Then share your feedback in groups.

1 - Strongly Disagree, 2 - Disagree, 3 - Agree, 4 - Strongly Agree	1	2	3	4
The presenter asked questions to involve the audience.				
The presenter looked at the audience while speaking.				
The presenter showed confidence in voice and body language.				
The presenter spoke clearly.				
The presenter explained ideas clearly.				

Total: _____

Suggest 3 ways the presenter might improve his or her future presentations.

1 _____

2 _____

3 _____

UNIT 3

EVALUATION FORM: Using signal phrases

Use this form to evaluate your classmates' presentations. Then share your feedback in groups.

1 - Strongly Disagree, 2 - Disagree, 3 - Agree, 4 - Strongly Agree	1	2	3	4
The presenter looked at the audience while speaking and involved the audience with questions.				
The presenter showed confidence in voice and body language.				
The presenter spoke clearly.				
The presenter used signal phrases to introduce ideas.				
The presenter explained ideas clearly.				

Total: _____

Suggest 3 ways the presenter might improve his or her future presentations.

1 _____

2 _____

3 _____

UNIT 4

EVALUATION FORM: Controlling speech speed

Use this form to evaluate your classmates' presentations. Then share your feedback in groups.

1 - Strongly Disagree, 2 - Disagree, 3 - Agree, 4 - Strongly Agree	1	2	3	4
The presenter looked at the audience and showed confidence in voice and body language.				
The presenter spoke at a comfortable speed.				
The presenter paused after important ideas.				
The presenter spoke clearly.				
The presenter explained ideas clearly.				

Total: _____

Suggest 3 ways the presenter might improve his or her future presentations.

1 _____

2 _____

3 _____

UNIT 5

EVALUATION FORM: Using visual aids

Use this form to evaluate your classmates' presentations. Then share your feedback in groups.

1 - Strongly Disagree, 2 - Disagree, 3 - Agree, 4 - Strongly Agree	1	2	3	4
The presenter looked at the audience and showed confidence in voice and body language.				
The presenter spoke clearly and at a comfortable speed.				
The presenter used visual aids effectively.				
The presenter used phrases to refer to the visual aids.				
The presenter explained the ideas clearly.				

Total: _____

Suggest 3 ways the presenter might improve his or her future presentations.

1 _____

2 _____

3 _____

UNIT 6

EVALUATION FORM: Showing enthusiasm

Use this form to evaluate your classmates' presentations. Then share your feedback in groups.

1 - Strongly Disagree, 2 - Disagree, 3 - Agree, 4 - Strongly Agree	1	2	3	4
The presenter showed enthusiasm with facial expressions, body language, voice, and word choice.				
The presenter spoke clearly and at a comfortable speed.				
The presenter used signal phrases to introduce ideas.				
The presenter used descriptive details.				
The presenter explained ideas clearly.				

Total: _____

Suggest 3 ways the presenter might improve his or her future presentations.

1 _____

2 _____

3 _____

UNIT 7

EVALUATION FORM: Giving a group presentation

Use this form to evaluate your classmates' presentations. Then share your feedback in groups.

1 - Strongly Disagree, 2 - Disagree, 3 - Agree, 4 - Strongly Agree	1	2	3	4
Each person in the group presented one section of the presentation.				
The presenters made transitions between speakers.				
The presenters showed enthusiasm.				
The presenters spoke clearly and at a comfortable speed.				
The presenters explained ideas clearly.				

Total: _____

Suggest 3 ways the presenters might improve their future presentations.

1 _____

2 _____

3 _____

UNIT 8

EVALUATION FORM: Comparing and contrasting

Use this form to evaluate your classmates' presentations. Then share your feedback in groups.

1 - Strongly Disagree, 2 - Disagree, 3 - Agree, 4 - Strongly Agree	1	2	3	4
The presenter used phrases of contrast to compare and contrast.				
The presenter showed contrast with stress and gestures.				
The presenter showed enthusiasm.				
The presenter spoke clearly and at a comfortable speed.				
The presenter explained the ideas clearly.				

Total: _____

Suggest 3 ways the presenter might improve his or her future presentations.

1 _____

2 _____

3 _____

UNIT 9

EVALUATION FORM: Describing a process

Use this form to evaluate your classmates' presentations. Then share your feedback in groups.

1 - Strongly Disagree, 2 - Disagree, 3 - Agree, 4 - Strongly Agree	1	2	3	4
The presenter described each phase of a process.				
The presenter explained the process clearly using sequencing expressions.				
The presenter showed enthusiasm.				
The presenter spoke clearly and at a comfortable speed.				
The presenter used visual aids effectively.				

Total: _____

Suggest 3 ways the presenter might improve his or her future presentations.

1 _____

2 _____

3 _____

UNIT 10

EVALUATION FORM: Telling a story

Use this form to evaluate your classmates' presentations. Then share your feedback in groups.

1 - Strongly Disagree, 2 - Disagree, 3 - Agree, 4 - Strongly Agree	1	2	3	4
The presenter spoke clearly and at a comfortable speed.				
The presenter used visual aids effectively.				
The presenter told a story using time and sequencing expressions.				
The presenter used the past tense to describe events in the past.				
The presenter explained the ideas clearly.				

Total: _____

Suggest 3 ways the presenter might improve his or her future presentations.

1 _____

2 _____

3 _____

UNIT 11

EVALUATION FORM: Pausing between ideas

Use this form to evaluate your classmates' presentations. Then share your feedback in groups.

1 - Strongly Disagree, 2 - Disagree, 3 - Agree, 4 - Strongly Agree	1	2	3	4
The presenter showed enthusiasm.				
The presenter paused between ideas and at the ends of sentences.				
The presenter spoke clearly and at a comfortable speed.				
The presenter used signal phrases to introduce ideas.				
The presenter explained the ideas clearly.				

Total: _____

Suggest 3 ways the presenter might improve his or her future presentations.

1 _____

2 _____

3 _____

UNIT 12

EVALUATION FORM: Introducing and concluding your presentation

Use this form to evaluate your classmates' presentations. Then share your feedback in groups.

1 - Strongly Disagree, 2 - Disagree, 3 - Agree, 4 - Strongly Agree	1	2	3	4
The presenter got my attention and introduced the topic.				
The presenter spoke clearly and at a comfortable speed.				
The presenter used signal phrases and pauses to introduce ideas.				
The presenter explained the ideas clearly.				
The presenter concluded the presentation with an important point and a question.				

Total: _____

Suggest 3 ways the presenter might improve his or her future presentations.

1 _____

2 _____

3 _____

Notes and Assignments

Photo Credits